CAMBRIDGE
Primary Science

Teacher's Resource 2

Jon Board & Alan Cross

CAMBRIDGE
UNIVERSITY PRESS

Shaftesbury Road, Cambridge CB2 8EA, United Kingdom

One Liberty Plaza, 20th Floor, New York, NY 10006, USA

477 Williamstown Road, Port Melbourne, VIC 3207, Australia

314–321, 3rd Floor, Plot 3, Splendor Forum, Jasola District Centre,
New Delhi – 110025, India

103 Penang Road, #05–06/07, Visioncrest Commercial, Singapore 238467

Cambridge University Press is part of the University of Cambridge.

It furthers the University's mission by disseminating knowledge in the pursuit of
education, learning and research at the highest international levels of excellence.

www.cambridge.org
Information on this title: www.cambridge.org/9781108785068

© Cambridge University Press & Assessment 2021

First published 2019
Second edition 2021

20 19 18 17 16 15 14 13 12 11 10 9 8 7 6 5

Printed in Poland by Opolgraf

A catalogue record for this publication is available from the British Library

ISBN 978-1-108-78506-8 Paperback with Digital access

Cambridge University Press has no responsibility for the persistence or accuracy of URLs
for external or third-party internet websites referred to in this publication, and does not
guarantee that any content on such websites is, or will remain, accurate or appropriate.
Information regarding prices, travel timetables, and other factual information given in
this work is correct at the time of first printing but Cambridge University Press does not
guarantee the accuracy of such information thereafter.

Cambridge International copyright material in this publication is reproduced under licence
and remains the intellectual property of Cambridge Assessment International Education.

Test-style questions [and sample answers] have been written by the authors. In Cambridge
Checkpoint tests or Cambridge Progression tests, the way marks are awarded may be
different. References to assessment and/or assessment preparation are the publisher's
interpretation of the curriculum framework requirements and may not fully reflect the
approach of Cambridge Assessment International Education.

Third-party websites and resources referred to in this publication have not been endorsed by
Cambridge Assessment International Education.

〉 Contents

Digital resources

The following items are available on Cambridge GO. For more information on how to access and use your digital resource, please see inside front cover.

Active learning

Assessment for Learning

Developing learner language skills

Differentiation

Improving learning through questioning

Language awareness

Metacognition

Skills for Life

Letter for parents – Introducing the Cambridge Primary resources

Lesson plan template and examples of completed lesson plans

Curriculum framework correlation

Scheme of work

Diagnostic check and answers

Answers to Learner's Book questions

Answers to Workbook questions

Glossary

You can download the following resources for each unit:

Differentiated worksheets and answers

Language worksheets and answers

Resource sheets

〉 Acknowledgements

Thanks to the following for permission to reproduce images:

Cover illustration by Omar Aranda (Beehive Illustration); *Inside Unit 6* Mimilopez/Getty Images

> Introduction

Welcome to the new edition of our Cambridge Primary Science series.

Since its launch, the series has been used by teachers and learners in over 100 countries for teaching the Cambridge Primary Science curriculum framework (0097) from 2020.

This exciting new edition has been designed by talking to Primary Science teachers all over the world. We have worked hard to understand your needs and challenges, and then carefully designed and tested the best ways of meeting them.

As a result of this research, we've made some important changes to the series. This Teacher's Resource has been carefully redesigned to make it easier for you to plan and teach the course.

The series still has extensive digital and online support, including Digital Classroom which lets you share books with your class and play videos and audio. This Teacher's Resource also offers additional materials available to download from Cambridge GO. (For more information on how to access and use your digital resource, please see inside front cover.)

The series uses the most successful teaching pedagogies like active learning and metacognition, and this Teacher's Resource gives you full guidance on how to integrate them into your classroom.

Formative assessment opportunities help you to get to know your learners better, with clear learning objectives and success criteria as well as an array of assessment techniques, including advice on self and peer assessment.

Clear, consistent differentiation ensures that all learners are able to progress in the course with tiered activities, differentiated worksheets and advice about supporting learners' different needs.

All our resources are written for teachers and learners who use English as a second or additional language. They help learners build core English skills with vocabulary and grammar support, as well as additional language worksheets.

We hope you enjoy using this course.

Eddie Rippeth

Head of Primary and Lower Secondary Publishing, Cambridge University Press

> About the authors

Jon Board

Jon Board is a lecturer in teacher training at the University of Manchester and also works as a specialist teacher of primary science at Mauldeth Road Primary School, Manchester. He has been teaching for 20 years and working in teacher training for more than 15 years. He also works internationally in teacher training, assessment and curriculum development, and has worked with teachers, education experts and education ministries in many countries including Egypt, Kazakhstan, Mongolia, Saudi Arabia, Macedonia and Indonesia. In addition to Cambridge Primary Science, Jon is the co-author of *Creative Ways to Teach Primary Science* published by McGraw Hill and of *Curious Learners in Primary Maths, Science, Computing and Design Technology*, published by Sage.

Jon is passionate about developing learners' curiosity by creating opportunities for them to ask and explore their own questions and about engaging learners in scientific thinking by getting them involved in planning and leading their own practical scientific enquiry. He is particularly interested in using primary science to develop learners' creative and rational problem-solving skills. These transferable, life-long skills will then be used in other subjects and in everyday situations. Cambridge Primary Science is written specifically to support teachers in developing this range of skills in learners as well as teaching the new vocabulary and the underpinning science knowledge required to do well in academic assessments.

Alan Cross

Alan has worked very successfully as a primary teacher, local advisor, trainer, inspector, external examiner, school governor and teacher educator. He has worked in the school and University sector in the UK and on projects and training around the world. Alan has researched primary STEM and has contributed to conferences and published extensively for teachers in primary science and technology including links with mathematics.

He loves to see curiosity and creativity develop in learners and teachers. Alan sees science as an amazing subject for opening people's eyes to the beauty of the universe including planet Earth. For him, science gives primary teachers the opportunity to introduce young minds to phenomena and explanations so that learners see another way to interact with the world, a way in which they can pose their own questions and begin to solve them.

Cambridge Primary Science provides the support that teachers need in empowering their learners' exploration and investigation of the world. Its stimulating materials and careful guidance give teachers confidence. Science tasks and activities are tried and tested and give a very strong emphasis to learners' primary classrooms

> How to use this series

All of the components in the series are designed to work together.

The Learner's Book is designed for learners to use in class with guidance from the teacher. It offers complete coverage of the curriculum framework. A variety of investigations, activities, questions and images motivate students and help them to develop the necessary scientific skills. Each unit contains opportunities for formative assessment, differentiation and reflection so you can support your learners' needs and help them progress.

The Teacher's Resource is the foundation of this series and you'll find everything you need to deliver the course in here, including suggestions for differentiation, formative assessment and language support, teaching ideas, answers and extra worksheets. Each Teacher's Resource includes:

- A **print book** with detailed teaching notes for each topic.
- **Digital Access** with all the material from the book in digital form plus editable planning documents, extra guidance, worksheets and more.

The skills-focused write-in Workbook provides further practice of all the topics in the Learner's Book and is ideal for use in class or as homework. A three-tier, scaffolded approach to skills development promotes visible progress and enables independent learning, ensuring that every learner is supported. Teachers can assign learners questions from one or more tiers for each exercise, or learners can progress through each of the tiers in the exercise.

Digital Classroom includes digital versions of the Learner's Book and Workbook, complete with pop-up answers, designed for teachers to use at the front of class. Easily share the books with the whole class on your whiteboard, zoom in, highlight and annotate text, and get your learners talking with videos, images and interactive activities

A letter to parents, explaining the course, is available to download from Cambridge GO (as part of this Teacher's Resource).

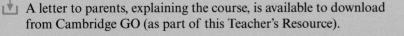

> How to use this Teacher's Resource

This Teacher's Resource contains both general guidance and teaching notes that help you to deliver the content in our Cambridge Primary Science resources. Some of the material is provided as downloadable files, available on **Cambridge GO**. (For more information about how to access and use your digital resource, please see inside front cover.) See the Contents page for details of all the material available to you, both in this book and through Cambridge GO.

Teaching notes

This book provides **teaching notes** for each unit of the Learner's Book and Workbook. Each set of teaching notes contains the following features to help you deliver the unit.

The **Unit plan** summarises the topics covered in the unit, including the number of learning hours recommended for the topic, an outline of the learning content and the Cambridge resources that can be used to deliver the topic.

Topic	Approximate number of learning hours	Outline of learning content	Resources
1.1 Habitats	2+	All about the local environment and some of the habitats where animals and plants live	**Learner's Book:** Activity: Habitat for a frog Think like a scientist 1: A habitat for fish Think like a scientist 2: Looking at habitats **Workbook:** Topic 1.1 **Digital Classroom:** Song – What lives here?

The **Background knowledge** feature explains prior knowledge required to access the unit and gives suggestions for addressing any gaps in your learners' prior knowledge.

Learners' prior knowledge can be informally assessed through the **Getting started** feature in the Learner's Book.

The **Teaching skills focus** feature covers a teaching skill and suggests how to implement it in the unit.

BACKGROUND KNOWLEDGE

When teaching Stage 2 learners about habitats in the local environment, you need to be clear about the terms home, habitat and environment. Environment usually refers to the wider surroundings in an area or district, including features of the land, atmosphere and the local plant and animal populations.

TEACHING SKILLS FOCUS

Active learning

Allow learners to make choices

It is important in science that learners make choices about activities and investigations. Can they select equipment?

Reflecting the Learner's Book, each unit consists of multiple sections. A section covers a learning topic.

At the start of each section, the **Learning plan** table includes the learning objectives, learning intentions and success criteria that are covered in the section.

It can be helpful to share learning intentions and success criteria with your learners at the start of a lesson so that they can begin to take responsibility for their own learning

LEARNING PLAN

Learning objectives	Learning intentions	Success criteria
2Be.01 Know that an environment in which a plant or animal naturally lives is its habitat.	• We are going to explore the environment to find the habitat of a living thing.	• I can explore the environment to find the habitat of a living thing.

There are often **common misconceptions** associated with particular learning topics. These are listed, along with suggestions for identifying evidence of the misconceptions in your class and suggestions for how to overcome them.

Misconception	How to identify	How to overcome
The words habitat and environment mean the same thing.	You may overhear this when you ask learners to talk together or talk to the class about the place an animal or plant lives.	Encourage learners to think of a large area as an environment and, within it, the place a living thing lives is its habitat.

For each topic, there is a selection of **starter ideas**, **main teaching ideas** and **plenary ideas**. You can pick out individual ideas and mix and match them depending on the needs of your class. The activities include suggestions for how they can be differentiated or used for assessment. **Homework ideas** are also provided.

Starter idea

1 What is the habitat of a ...?
(10–15 minutes)

Resources: Nine cards, each with the name of a habitat written on it. For example, tree, pond, river, forest, seashore, sea, desert, field, mountain, Workbook 1.1 Focus (optional)

Description: Explain that this is a game, that one person says the name of an animal and another has to point to the word for its habitat. Check that everyone is familiar with the habitats.

Main teaching ideas

1 Activity: Habitat for a frog
(30 minutes)

Learning intentions: We are going to explore a local environment to find the habitat of a living thing.

We are going to make observations and record them in drawings.

Resources: Learner's Book, Workbook 1.1 Challenge (optional) Digital Classroom song: What lives here? (optional)

Description: Read the description of the activity in the Learner's Book. Learners might look at the picture of the frog on the lily pad in the Learner's Book Topic 1.1.

The **Language support** feature contains suggestions for how to support learners with English as an additional language. The vocabulary terms and definitions from the Learner's Book are also collected here.

LANGUAGE SUPPORT

The first three topics in this unit deal with local environments and habitats. This means that some of the language used will be familiar when learners talk about local features, for example, parks, gardens, trees, etc.

The **Cross-curricular links** feature provides suggestions for linking to other subject areas.

CROSS-CURRICULAR LINKS

This topic links strongly to environmental education and to geography because it is about the features of different places and the animals and plants that grow in these places. As many of the activities require drawing, there are also links to art.

> **Digital Classroom:** If you have access to Digital Classroom, these links will suggest when to use the various multimedia enhancements and interactive activities.

Digital resources to download

This Teacher's Resource includes a range of digital materials that you can download from Cambridge GO. (For more information about how to access and use your digital resource, please see inside front cover.) This icon ⬇ indicates material that is available from Cambridge GO.

Helpful documents for planning include:

- **Letter for parents – Introducing the Cambridge Primary resources:** a template letter for parents, introducing the Cambridge Primary Science resources.
- **Lesson plan template:** a Word document that you can use for planning your lessons. Examples of completed lesson plans are also provided.
- **Curriculum framework correlation:** a table showing how the Cambridge Primary Science resources map to the Cambridge Primary Science curriculum framework.
- **Scheme of work:** a suggested scheme of work that you can use to plan teaching throughout the year.

Each unit includes:

- **Differentiated worksheets:** these worksheets are provided in variations that cater for different abilities. Worksheets labelled 'A' are intended to support less confident learners, worksheets labelled 'B' should cater for the majority of learners, while worksheets labelled 'C' are designed to challenge more confident learners. Answer sheets are provided.
- **Language worksheets:** these worksheets provide language support and can be particularly helpful for learners with English as an additional language.
- **Resource sheets:** these include templates and any other materials that support activities described in the teaching notes.

Additionally, the Teacher's Resource includes:

- **Diagnostic check and answers:** a test to use at the beginning of the year to discover the level that learners are working at. The results of this check can inform your planning.
- **Answers to Learner's Book questions**
- **Answers to Workbook questions**
- **Glossary**

In addition, you can find more detailed information about teaching approaches.

▶ **Video** is available through the Digital Classroom.

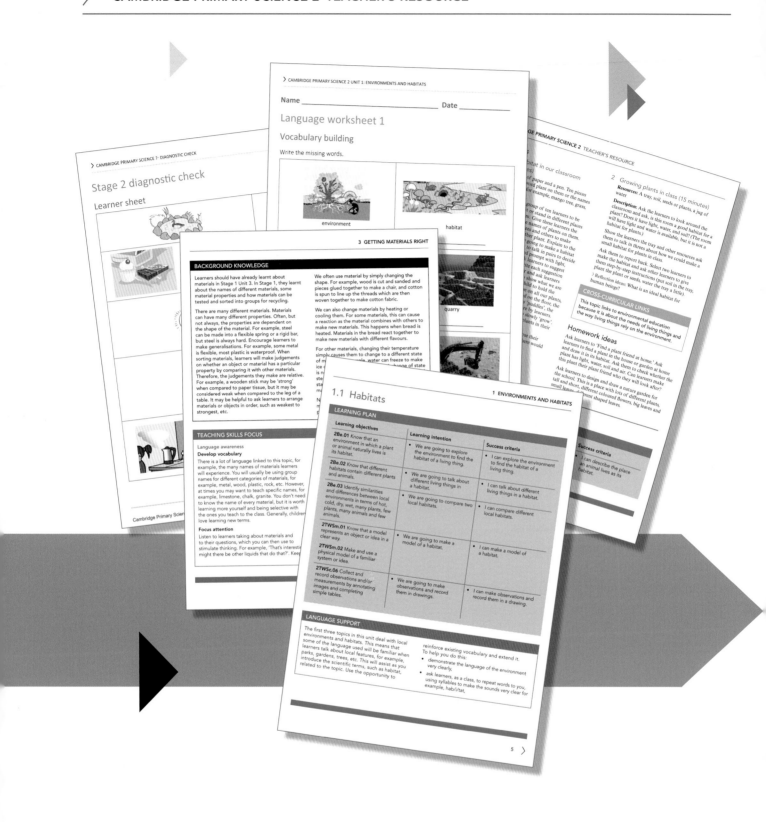

> About the curriculum framework

The information in this section is based on the Cambridge Primary Science curriculum framework (0097) from 2020. You should always refer to the appropriate curriculum framework document for the year of your learners' assessment to confirm the details and for more information. Visit ***www.cambridgeinternational.orglprimary*** *to find out more.*

The Cambridge Primary Science curriculum framework has been updated for teaching from September 2021. The Primary Science curriculum framework has been developed to support learners in building their understanding about the natural world, particularly how to explain and investigate phenomena.

The curriculum framework incorporates three components:

- four content strands (Biology, Chemistry, Physics, and Earth and Space)
- a skills strand called Thinking and Working Scientifically
- a context strand called Science in Context.

Biology, Chemistry, Physics and Earth and Space provide the scientific knowledge content, which gradually develops from stage 1 to stage 6 and provides a smooth progression towards Cambridge Lower Secondary study.

The Thinking and Working Scientifically learning objectives focus on the key scientific skills that are developed throughout the course. This strand is split into five types of scientific enquiry:

- observing over time
- identifying and classifying
- pattern seeking
- fair testing
- research.

Science in Context allows for personal, local and global contexts to be incorporated into scientific study, making science relevant to the contexts that learners are familiar with. This element of the curriculum framework offers great flexibility to teachers and learners around the world.

The Cambridge Primary Science curriculum framework promotes a learner-led, enquiry-based approach. Practical work is a valuable part of science learning and develops learners' investigation skills such as observation, measurement and equipment handling.

❯ About the assessment

Information about the assessment of the Cambridge Primary Science curriculum framework is available on the Cambridge Assessment International Education website. https://www.cambridgeinternational.org/primary

❯ Approaches to learning and teaching

The following are the key pedagogies underpinning our course content and how we understand and define them.

Active learning

Active learning is a pedagogical practice that places student learning at its centre. It focuses on how students learn, not just on what they learn. We, as teachers, need to encourage learners to 'think hard', rather than passively receive information. Active learning encourages learners to take responsibility for their learning and supports them in becoming independent and confident learners in school and beyond.

Assessment for Learning

Assessment for Learning (AfL) is a teaching approach that generates feedback which can be used to improve learners' performance. Learners become more involved in the learning process and, from this, gain confidence in what they are expected to learn and to what standard. We, as teachers, gain insights into a learner's level of understanding of a particular concept or topic, which helps to inform how we support their progression.

Differentiation

Differentiation is usually presented as a teaching practice where teachers think of learners as individuals and learning as a personalised process. Whilst precise definitions can vary, typically the core aim of differentiation is viewed as ensuring that all learners, no matter their ability, interest or context, make progress towards their learning outcomes.

It is about using different approaches and appreciating the differences in learners to help them make progress. Teachers therefore need to be responsive, and willing and able to adapt their teaching to meet the needs of their learners.

Language awareness

For many learners, English is an additional language. It might be their second or perhaps their third language. Depending on the school context, students might be learning all or just some of their subjects through English.

For all learners, regardless of whether they are learning through their first language or an additional language, language is a vehicle for learning. It is through language that students access the learning intentions of the lesson and communicate their ideas. It is our responsibility, as teachers, to ensure that language doesn't present a barrier to learning.

Metacognition

Metacognition describes the processes involved when learners plan, monitor, evaluate and make changes to their own learning behaviours. These processes help learners to think about their own learning more explicitly and ensure that they are able to meet a learning goal that they have identified themselves or that we, as teachers, have set.

Skills for life

How do we prepare learners to succeed in a fast-changing world? To collaborate with people from around the globe? To create innovation as technology increasingly takes over routine work? To use advanced thinking skills in the face of more complex challenges? To show resilience in the face of constant change? At Cambridge, we are responding to educators who have asked for a way to understand how all these different approaches to life skills and competencies relate to their teaching. We have grouped these skills into six main Areas of Competency that can be incorporated into teaching, and have examined the different stages of the learning journey and how these competencies vary across each stage.

These six key areas are:

• Creativity – finding new ways of doing things, and solutions to problems

• Collaboration – the ability to work well with others

• Communication – speaking and presenting confidently and participating effectively in meetings

• Critical thinking – evaluating what is heard or read, and linking ideas constructively

• Learning to learn – developing the skills to learn more effectively

• Social responsibilities – contributing to social groups, and being able to talk to and work with people from other cultures.

Excerpts have been taken from the *Approaches to learning and teaching* series, courtesy of Cambridge University Press and Cambridge Assessment International Education: cambridge.org/approachestolearning

Cambridge learner and teacher attributes

This course helps develop the following Cambridge learner and teacher attributes.

Cambridge teachers	Cambridge learners
Confident in teaching their subject and engaging each student in learning.	**Confident** in working with information and ideas – their own and those of others.
Responsible for themselves, responsive to and respectful of others.	**Responsible** for themselves, responsive to and respectful of others.
Reflective as learners themselves, developing their practice.	**Reflective** as learners, developing their ability to learn.
Innovative and equipped for new and future challenges.	**Innovative** and equipped for new and future challenges.
Engaged intellectually, professionally and socially, ready to make a difference.	**Engaged** intellectually and socially, ready to make a difference.

Reproduced from Developing the Cambridge learner attributes *with permission from Cambridge Assessment International Education.*

More information about these approaches to learning and teaching is available to download from Cambridge GO (as part of this Teacher's Resource).

⟩ Setting up for success

Our aim is to support better learning in the classroom with resources that allow for increased learner autonomy while supporting teachers to facilitate student learning.

Through an active learning approach of enquiry-led tasks, open-ended questions and opportunities to externalise thinking in a variety of ways, learners will develop analysis, evaluation and problem-solving skills.

Some ideas to consider to encourage an active learning environment are as follows:

- Set up seating to make group work easy.
- Create classroom routines to help learners to transition between different types of activity efficiently, e.g. move from pair work to listening to the teacher to independent work.
- Source mini-whiteboards, which allow you to get feedback from all learners rapidly.
- Start a portfolio for each learner, keeping key pieces of work to show progress at parent–teacher days.
- Have a display area with learner work and vocab flashcards.

Planning for active learning

We recommend the following approach to planning.

1 **Plan learning intentions and success criteria:** these are the most important feature of the lesson. Teachers and learners need to know where they are going in order to plan a route to get there.

2 **Plan language support:** think about strategies to help learners overcome the language demands of the lesson so that language doesn't present a barrier to learning.

3 **Plan starter activities:** include a 'hook' or starter to engage learners using imaginative strategies. This should be an activity where all learners are active from the start of the lesson.

4 **Plan main activities:** during the lesson, try to: give clear instructions, with modelling and written support; coordinate logical and orderly transitions between activities; make sure that learning is active and all learners are engaged; create opportunities for discussion around key concepts.

5 **Plan assessment for learning and differentiation:** use a wide range of Assessment for Learning techniques and adapt activities to a wide range of abilities. Address misconceptions at appropriate points and give meaningful oral and written feedback which learners can act on.

6 **Plan reflection and plenary:** at the end of each activity and at the end of each lesson, try to: ask learners to reflect on what they have learnt compared to the beginning of the lesson; build on and extend this learning.

7 **Plan homework:** if setting homework, it can be used to consolidate learning from the previous lesson or to prepare for the next lesson.

To help planning using this approach, a blank Lesson plan template is available to download from Cambridge GO (as part of this Teacher's Resource). There are also examples of completed lesson plans.

For more guidance on setting up for success and planning, please explore the Professional Development pages of our website **www.cambridge.org/education/PD**

> 1 Environments and habitats

Unit plan

Topic	Approximate number of learning hours	Outline of learning content	Resources
1.1 Habitats	2+	All about the local environment and some of the habitats where animals and plants live.	**Learner's Book:** Activity: Habitat for a frog Think like a scientist 1: A habitat for fish Think like a scientist 2: Looking at habitats **Workbook:** Topic 1.1 **Digital Classroom:** Song – What lives here?
1.2 Plants in different habitats	2+	Observation of different habitats for plants.	**Learner's Book:** Think like a scientist 1: Plants in different habitats Activity: Find me a habitat Think like a scientist 2: Finding all the plants in a habitat **Workbook:** Topic 1.2
1.3 Animals in different habitats	2+	Observation of different habitats for animals.	**Learner's Book:** Think like a scientist: Habitats for animals around school Activity 1: A habitat for snails Activity 2: Let's make an insect hotel **Workbook:** Topic 1.3

Topic	Approximate number of learning hours	Outline of learning content	Resources
1.4 Rocks and the environment	2+	About the features of rocks and how we extract them.	**Learner's Book:** Think like a scientist 1: Learning more about rocks Think like a scientist 2: Does this rock absorb water? Think like a scientist 3: Sorting stones with water **Workbook:** Topic 1.4 **Digital Classroom:** Video – How do we dig up rocks? Science Investigators Video – What are rocks used for?
1.5 How can we care for our environment?	2+	How we care for the environment to help animals and plants.	**Learner's Book:** Activity 1: Litter and pollution Activity 2: Making a nature reserve Think like a scientist: Survey the local environment **Workbook:** Topic 1.5 ⬇ Worksheets 1.5A, 1.5B, 1.5C

Across unit resources

Learner's Book:

Project: Our school's outdoor environment

Check your progress quiz

Teacher's Resource:

⬇ Language worksheets 1 and 2

⬇ Stage 2 Diagnostic check

Digital Classroom:

⬇ End-of-unit quiz

BACKGROUND KNOWLEDGE

When teaching Stage 2 learners about habitats in the local environment, you need to be clear about the terms home, habitat and environment. Environment usually refers to the wider surroundings in an area or district, including features of the land, atmosphere and the local plant and animal populations. The term habitat refers specifically to the area in which the plant or animals lives, for example, a grass plant may live by a wall or a tree, this is its habitat; a mouse might live in a field and a nearby area of trees, this its habitat. Take care with the term home. It is sometimes used instead of the word habitat, but people often use it to name of the place that the animal regularly shelters or sleeps, for example, the nest of a bird, the burrow of a rabbit, the den of a bear, the lair of a wolf. Of course, many animals do not have such a 'home', for example, many fish, many insects.

CONTINUED

Be aware that when studying habitats in the primary school setting it is easier to find plants than animals. Animals tend to be scared by groups of learners and so will hide or move away.

When talking to learners about the habitat of human beings it is not so easy to refer to a single habitat. This is because humans alter their clothing or shelters to suit the environment. For example, we build and heat homes in very cold parts of planet Earth. Make sure you can talk about a range of animals and their habitats, for example, a crab on the shore, a bird in a forest, a frog in and by a pond.

You may find it useful to have some books or posters to help you and the learners identify common animals and plants. If some of these books are designed to be used by children, this is even better. It is not essential that you know the names of plants and animals. It is more important that you can recognise a wide range of animals and plants and that you are able to make careful observations, for example, of body shape, body colours, number of legs, and use books etc to identify animals and plants.

Make yourself aware of any local animals that are venomous or that bite. Check if there are areas to avoid such as habitats near water. You must take extra precautions if you plan to take learners close to open water. For example, you should have more adult helpers. Always take advice from school colleagues about safety.

Be aware that in some places it is illegal to collect plants from the wild (not in a cultivated garden). Tell learners that they should respect living things and, even when doing science, we always care for living things.

TEACHING SKILLS FOCUS

As a teacher of Stage 2 you will find that learners learn best by talking, doing and thinking. This unit is ideal because learners have experienced the local environment which you can access by stepping into the school grounds or, if this is not possible, viewing the grounds from school windows.

Active learning

Allow learners to make choices

It is important in science that learners make choices about activities and investigations. Can they select equipment? Can they choose who they work with? Can they choose ways to record results and more? You will find that as learners become more independent, you have more time to focus on supporting different learners.

Ensure that learners are active thinkers

When learners make choices, ask them to explain why they want to do one thing or another. When they are observing something new, teach them to ask questions beginning with how…?, why…? when…?, where…?, who…? Use these question starters yourself but encourage learners to ask their own questions and to seek answers.

Misconceptions

The terms home, habitat and environment may need clarification because learners often confuse them. Begin with plants, which tend to have a small habitat and familiar animals with a small habitat, for example, frog, earthworm, snail, fish living in a pond. Later contrast this with larger habitats, for example, a wolf or bear may roam over many miles as do some birds, for example, an eagle.

Your reflection

Your awareness of possible learner misconceptions will assist your teaching as it will help you anticipate possible difficulties for some learners. For example, many learners assume that all animals have a 'bed' of some kind and a 'home' of some kind.

Make sure you focus part of each lesson on Thinking and Working Scientifically, for example, skills of observation or using a table. Reflect on the effect this has on learners. Do their skills improve? Does this assist their learning of science?

1.1 Habitats

LEARNING PLAN

Learning objectives	Learning intention	Success criteria
2Be.01 Know that an environment in which a plant or animal naturally lives is its habitat.	• We are going to explore the environment to find the habitat of a living thing.	• I can explore the environment to find the habitat of a living thing.
2Be.02 Know that different habitats contain different plants and animals.	• We are going to talk about different living things in a habitat.	• I can talk about different living things in a habitat.
2Be.03 Identify similarities and differences between local environments in terms of hot, cold, dry, wet, many plants, few plants, many animals and few animals.	• We are going to compare two local habitats.	• I can compare different local habitats.
2TWSm.01 Know that a model represents an object or idea in a clear way. **2TWSm.02** Make and use a physical model of a familiar system or idea.	• We are going to make a model of a habitat.	• I can make a model of a habitat.
2TWSc.06 Collect and record observations and/or measurements by annotating images and completing simple tables.	• We are going to make observations and record them in drawings.	• I can make observations and record them in a drawing.

LANGUAGE SUPPORT

The first three topics in this unit deal with local environments and habitats. This means that some of the language used will be familiar when learners talk about local features, for example, parks, gardens, trees, etc. This will assist as you introduce the scientific terms, such as habitat, related to the topic. Use the opportunity to reinforce existing vocabulary and extend it. To help you do this:

• demonstrate the language of the environment very clearly,

• ask learners, as a class, to repeat words to you, using syllables to make the sounds very clear for example, hab/i/tat,

CONTINUED

- make a class poster of environmental words,
- make a class glossary poster where you give the meaning of words or an example sentence using the word,
- ask questions which encourage learners to use the words. for example, using the word habitat, tell me where the toad lives.

Language worksheets 1 and 2 are provided to assist learners with science vocabulary for this unit. Learners can copy the words on Language worksheet 1 and complete the sentences on Language worksheet 2. The Language worksheets can also be used as:

- posters on the classroom wall,
- a glossary in the Learner's Book,
- a prompt sheet on a learner's desk,
- a classroom display,
- words and pictures can be cut out and used in a matching game. For example, can you match the word or sentence to the picture?

compare: to look at two things and find things that are similar and different

environment: the natural and man-made space and things around you

habitat: the place a living thing finds everything it needs to grow and have young

home: the place an animal sleeps, feels safe and cares for its young

label: words added to a picture to give information

local: the area around you

model: a copy we make (often smaller) of a real thing

Common misconceptions

Misconception	How to identify	How to overcome
The words habitat and environment mean the same thing.	You may overhear this when you ask learners to talk together or talk to the class about the place an animal or plant lives.	Encourage learners to think of a large area as an environment and, within it, the place a living thing lives is its habitat.
Some learners may confuse the home of an animal with its habitat.	You may notice this if you ask learners to talk about animals and where they live.	Ask learners to talk about the place where an animal sleeps, for example, a nest or a burrow, and the place where it would find its food and water. Together these are the animal's habitat.
Learners may think that wild animals include only dangerous animals like wolves, tigers and lions, or that they only live far away in hard to reach places.	Ask learners about wild animals living around their home and school. They may respond and say that there are none.	Give learners examples of non-wild animals, for example, pets and farm animals. Explain that most other animals, for example, fish, birds, insects, look after themselves in cities, towns and natural environments. All these animals are wild.

Starter ideas

1 What is the habitat of a …? (10–15 minutes)

Resources: Nine cards, each with the name of a habitat written on it. For example, tree, pond, river, forest, seashore, sea, desert, field, mountain, Workbook 1.1 Focus (optional)

Description: Explain that this is a game, that one person says the name of an animal and another has to point to the word for its habitat. Check that everyone is familiar with the habitats. Demonstrate this with a learner. You say an animal, for example, a crab and the learner then points to seashore card.

Follow this up with the Workbook 1.1 Focus task which asks learners to identify living things in a habitat.

Check that learners are using the terms correctly, for example, habitat, and that they are not confusing the animals home with its habitat.

2 Plants living in a park or garden (10 minutes)

Description: Ask the learners if they have seen a park, a garden, a farm or a greenhouse. Explain that these are places made by people to help plants grow. Ask learners to talk in pairs about how the gardener or farmer makes the place just right for the plants to grow (for example, making sure plants have good soil, lots of light, water and fresh air). Ask some learners to report back to class and discuss their ideas. For example, why do the plants need light? This is how the plants make food in their leaves. Check that learners are not confusing home, habitat and environment. Encourage them to talk about different animals and their home, habitat and environment.

3 Different environments (10–15 minutes)

Resources: Learner's Book, Workbook 1.1 Practice (optional)

Description: Ask learners to look at the three photographs at the beginning of this topic. Ask learners to talk in pairs about each animal they can see and the local environment in which it lives. Ask learners to report back to class on the animal, name it and describe the animal's local environment. Ask learners to talk in pairs about each animal's needs (you could assign one animal to different pairs or they could discuss them all). For example, the eagle needs food, water, air, warmth, a place to build a

home and raise young (nest). Ask learners to report back.

You might then ask learners to complete the Workbook 1.1 Practice task where they compare two habitats.

Main teaching ideas

1 Activity: Habitat for a frog (30 minutes)

Learning intention: We are going to explore a local environment to find the habitat of a living thing.

We are going to make observations and record them in drawings.

Resources: Learner's Book, Workbook 1.1 Challenge (optional) Digital Classroom song: What lives here? (optional)

Description: Read the description of the activity in the Learner's Book. Learners might look at the picture of the frog on the lily pad in the Learner's Book Topic 1.1. Ask small groups of learners to imagine that they are a frog family and to think about the things they need, for example, a home (pond), water to drink and swim in, food (small insects living in or close to the pond). Ask a group to crouch at the front on the class and talk about the things they need. Ask the class in their groups to talk about the habitat the frogs will need (open water to swim in and find food, weeds to hide in, a beach or bank to hop onto, lots of insects to eat, deeper water to hide in). Remind learners that some animals want to eat frogs, for example, owls, storks, herons, snakes. Ask all learners to form more frog 'families', talk about their habitat and report back about an ideal frog habitat.

Ask learners to draw and label the ideal habitat for a frog. By the end of the activity, learners should understand the needs of a frog and that a frog needs a habitat that will provide these things.

Learners might be asked to complete Workbook 1.1 Challenge where they consider the needs of three living things and where these living things would find the things they need.

> **Digital Classroom:** If you have access to the Digital Classroom component, use the song 'What lives here?', either as an introduction or to follow the activity. Emphasise that living things are all different and each is suited to a particular environment. The i button will explain how to use the song.

> **Differentiation ideas:** If learners find these discussions difficult, put the examples (in brackets above) on to cards for them to use to give them ideas.

Challenge more confident learners by asking them to think of the needs of other animals in a pond habitat, for example, fish, birds.

> **Assessment ideas:** Assess whether learners understand the needs of frogs by asking learners to identify things that a frog does not need, for example, sweets, TV, etc.

2 Think like a scientist 1: A habitat for fish (30–40 minutes)

Learning intention: We are going to explore our local environment to find the habitat of a living thing.

We are going to make a model of a habitat.

Resources: Learner's Book, a shoe box or similar-sized box, card, paper, scissors, coloured pens, glue, and sticky tape

Description: Explain that, when we keep an animal as a pet, we should look after it well.

If the pet is a small animal, we can make a habitat for it to live in.

Ask your learners to look at the picture of the fish tank and what it contains, for example, gravel, water, weeds, rocks, water, fish. Ask learners to talk in pairs about what they have seen and any other fish tanks they may have seen. Explain that learners are going to make a model of a fish tank using paper and card. Ask learners, in pairs, to make a drawing of what they might make and then give each pair a box, paper and card so that they can make their model.

Explain to learners that they have made a model of a fish tank. Ask them in pairs to discuss and then share why a model like this is useful in science e.g. it is quick to make and change, we can see different parts, it helps us learn about a habitat that fish might like.

Ask learners to share their ideas with the group. What have they included? Why? Explain to learners that they have made a model of a fish tank. Ask them in pairs to discuss and then share why a model like this is useful in science e.g. it is quick to make and change, we can see different parts, it helps us learn about a habitat that fish might like.

> **Assessment ideas:** Ask learners to describe a day in the life of a fish, the things it will need and do.

3 Think like a scientist 2: Looking at habitats (30 minutes)

Learning intention: We are going to talk about different living things in a habitat.

We are going to compare two local habitats.

We are going to make observations and record them in drawings.

Resources: Learner's Book, access to an outdoor area (if this is not possible access to a window which overlooks an outdoor area, or to photographs taken in an outdoor area, or use a large planter with several plants growing in it, alternatively meet learners at the end of playtime outside and do the activity as you come into school).

Description: Read the description of the activity in the Learner's Book. Begin by asking learners to compare the two habitats illustrated in the Learner's Book. What similarities can they see? What differences can they see?

Then take your learners to a place where they can see an area of plants where animals may live or visit. Ask them in pairs to look carefully at the different plants and draw at least one plant. Ask them to look for very small plants, larger ones and the largest plants.

Ask learners to report back about the plants they have found. Ask them whether the plants are growing healthily. Ask learners what a plant needs to grow healthily (light, water, soil, air). Ask learners if this habitat is giving the plants the things they need. Ask learners to describe the habitat, for example, an area with several bushes, other plants, soil, light, air and water (the water will be in the damp soil underground).

If you have time, you might talk about animals which might live here (for example, insects like ants), this is their habitat, and animals which might visit this place, for example, birds. Then go to another area to compare the first environment with this one. Is the second area drier, wetter, more sunny? While outside, or back in class, ask the learners to draw the two habitats.

By the end of the activity, learners should see these spaces as habitats, but that habitats vary. They should understand that the habitat gives a plant all that it needs.

> **Practical guidance:** Check that no learners have allergies, for example, to pollen. Warn learners that they should not damage or scare any living things; not eat things found outside and wash their hands with soap and water after touching plants.

> **Differentiation ideas:** When reporting back in class, some confident learners may be asked to include some writing. For example, ask these learners to note some key words about the habitats such as dry, wet, dark. Less confident learners might be given more opportunity to talk and then draw. You might support them with cards displaying key words, for example, plants, trees, leaves, habitat, insect, bird.

> **Assessment ideas:** Ask a learner to write 1–4 on a piece of paper. Next to each number they should write or draw one thing that a plant needs to live.

Plenary ideas

1 Choosing a habitat (10–15 minutes)

Resources: Pairs of cards, one card in the pair features one word or phrase, the other card the other word in the pair. Pairs include: dry/wet, hot/cold, on land/in water, plants to eat/animals to eat.

Description: Explain that this is a game. You will name an animal and the learners must think about its habitat. For example, you might name a wild goat. Show the word pairs to the learners and ask them to choose one word from each pair that describes the animal's habitat. Put the rejected cards to one side each time. At the end you will have cards describing a suitable habitat. Repeat with other animals for example, a fish, a frog, a bird.

NB have some spare cards to hand to create more labels suggested by learners.

> **Reflection ideas:** Ask learners to think about an animal living in a habitat which is then destroyed or damaged by people. What will the animal do? What will happen to the plants?

2 Lots of seeds (10 minutes)

Description: Explain that even a small tree will make many seed each year. The seeds will be blown all around but they don't all grow. Can learners say why not? (Some land in places which are not a suitable habitat, for example, on a road.)

Ask learners to name places that would be bad for a seed to land, for example, a path of stones, a road, on the roof of a building, a river, inside a building, on dry sand, in a cave. Ask learners to explain why some of these are not good habitats for a plant. Make it clear that these are not good habitats for a plant. (In some there is no soil, little water, little light.) Remind learners that some seeds will land in a good habitat. Ask learners to talk in pairs about what makes a good habitat for a plant (light, water, soil, air) and then report back to the class. Learners should be clear that a plant will only grow healthily if its habitat provides the things it needs.

> **Reflection ideas:** Ask learners to think about a very large tree. Could another plant grow in that place? If not, why not? (There is no light.)

Homework ideas

Learners should draw part of a garden: this could be from their own home or that of a relative, or a public garden. They should draw in some of the plants as well as animals that might live there or visit this area.

Learners might be given an animal to think about. for example, a dolphin, an eagle, a bear. They should draw the animal and its habitat.

1.2 Plants in different habitats

LEARNING PLAN

Learning objectives	Learning intention	Success criteria
2Be.01 Know that an environment in which a plant or animal naturally lives is its habitat.	• We are going to describe the place a plant lives as its habitat.	• I can describe the place that a plant lives as its habitat.
2Be.02 Know that different habitats contain different plants and animals.	• We are going to describe different plants in a habitat.	• I can describe different living things in a habitat.
2Be.03 Identify similarities and differences between local environments in terms of hot, cold, dry, wet, many plants, few plants, many animals and few animals.	• We are going to compare different habitats for plants.	• I can compare different habitats for plants.
2TWSc.06 Collect and record observations and/or measurements by annotating images and completing simple tables.	• We are going to observe plants and record what we see in drawings and tables.	• I can observe things and record what I see in a drawings and tables.
2TWSc.02 Use given equipment appropriately.	• We are going to use a magnifying glass.	• I can use a magnifying glass.

LANGUAGE SUPPORT

In this topic, and the others in this unit, learners are asked to compare habitats, so be prepared to structure discussion around the language of comparison, for example, open questions such as: 'What do we see here?' Encourage learners to state a conclusion. For example, support statements beginning with: 'This habitat is …', 'In this habitat the plant has …'; 'Plants living here have… . Here are some further ideas.

• Make the learning of plant names a fun activity. For example, this plant is tall, it gives you shade, take care, the leaves are sharp, what is it? (A yucca)

• Ask learners to watch your lips and tongue as you say and repeat a word (and its syllables), for example, en/vi/ron/ment, then ask the learners to repeat it back to you.

• Add more words to a class poster of environmental words.

• Add more words to a class glossary poster where you give the meaning of words or an example sentence using the word.

Learners will usually find differences easier to identify than similarities. When you ask them to compare habitats, always ask for similarities, for example, there is light and water, as well as differences, for example, one is dry, the other is wet.

CONTINUED

crack: a broken part of a material

describe: use words to say what something is like

desert: a very dry place with very few or no living things

photograph: a picture made by a camera

pretend: imagine something

record: to draw or write what happened

Common misconceptions

Misconception	How to identify	How to overcome
Some learners may think that a plant can grow anywhere.	Ask learners to talk about a plant and the places it might grow locally. See if they can identify places it could not grow.	Suggest local habitats, suitable and not suitable for a plant. Would a plant grow in a flower bed? Would it grow on a road?

Starter ideas

1 Different habitats for plants (10 minutes)

Resources: Learner's Book

Description: Ask learners to look at the picture at the start of Topic 1.2. Ask learners to talk in pairs about the habitat, how the plants get water (through their roots from the river or from damp soil). Ask the learners to look for the plants growing in the hot desert. Ask them if these plants would be happy growing in the river? If not, why not. (A river gives too much water – a cactus is very good at growing in dry places where most plants will not grow.) Ask learners to think and talk about problems the plants might face in these habitats (for example, the desert may get too dry so there is no water underground; the river might dry up; after heavy rain the river will get very deep and fast). Explain that, because we can see lots of healthy plants in each picture, the habitat must be giving them what they need (light, water, soil and air).

This activity assists when learners think that any plant can grow anywhere. Point out that particular plants grow in particular places. For example, pond weed grows underwater in fresh water.

2 Plants growing in the same habitat (10–15 minutes)

Resources: Workbook 1.2 Focus (optional)

Description: Ask six children to join you at the front of the class, to curl up on the floor in a group (but about 30 cm apart) and pretend to be seeds. Explain that these seeds are lucky because that have fallen into a good habitat, lots of light, enough water in the soil and lots of fresh air. Tell the seeds to slowly start to grow, wriggle their toes, these are the roots, slowly stretch up an arm, then lift a head, rise to their feet, stretch out arms and hands as branches and leaves and their faces are beautiful flowers. Can the class see that they are all growing and sharing the habitat? Ask learners what will happen as they keep growing and get very big. Allow learners to discuss this. Will they have enough water and light? Might we find that some plants will grow well but others may not and may die? Ask learners what has happened. (As the plants grow, they need more and more light and the bigger ones will shade the others, so some plants may have difficulty in staying alive.)

At this point you might ask learners to complete Workbook 1.2 Focus where they are asked to draw a suitable habitat for a plant and circle the words to identify the requirements of a plant.

Learners may think that growth will be the same for each plant. They may not have considered that competition (for example, for light) may affect plants.

Main teaching ideas

1 Think like a scientist 1: Plants in different habitats (30–40 minutes)

Learning intention: We are going to describe different plants in a habitat.

We are going to compare different habitats for plants.

We are going to observe plants and record what we see in drawings and tables.

Resources: Learner's Book, access to an outdoor area (if this is not possible, access to a window which overlooks an outdoor area, or to photographs taken in an outdoor area, or use a large planter with several plants growing in it, alternatively meet your class at the end of playtime outside and do the activity as you come into school), camera (optional), Workbook 1.2 Practice (optional), clipboards (optional)

Description: Read the description of the activity in the Learner's Book. Take your learners to a place where they can see plants growing in different places, for example, in a flower bed, in a path or wall, in a planter, in a wet place, in a dry place.

Explain that plants will grow if the seed falls in a good habitat (enough light, water, soil and air).

Take the class to a place where they can observe plants growing.

Ask some learners to point to a plant and tell the class where it is growing and if it has all the things it needs to grow (light, water, soil and air).

Ask learners about what happens to seeds that land in an unsuitable habitat (they do not grow).

Ask learners to draw a plant growing in its habitat.

Back in class, they can complete a record like the one in the Learner's Book.

Ask the learners to look at the records made by other learners and see that plants grow in different habitats. To do this ask every learner to stand up, hold their record, then move around the room. When you call stop, they must pair up with the nearest person and share the plant they found and its habitat. Repeat this once or twice. Finish the lesson with a reminder of the range of plants and habitats seen and that every living thing needs the right habitat.

At this point you might ask learners to complete the Workbook 1.2 Practice exercise, where they are asked to design the habitat for a plant inside a greenhouse.

> **Practical guidance:** If you cannot take learners out of doors, take them to a window or windows to observe plants outside. You might also show them photographs taken of different plant habitats around the site, for example, a dry area, a wet area, a very sunny area, a dark area, plants growing in unusual places.

Check that no learners have allergies e.g. to pollen. Warn learners that they should not damage or scare any living things; not eat things found outside and wash their hands with soap and water after touching plants.

> **Differentiation ideas:** Observe the learners when they are observing plants and making records. If they appear to lack confidence, support them back in class with vocabulary or prompts 'you need to drink every day, are plants the same in this way?'.

Challenge more confident learners by asking them to think about a different habitat, for example, a hot desert. What difficulties might a plant face?

> **Assessment ideas:** Observe and listen to learners when they talk about the plants observed and the habitat. Can the learners describe the features that a plant needs?

2 Activity: Find me a habitat (15 minutes)

Learning intention: We are going to describe the place a plant lives as its habitat.

We are going to compare different habitats for plants.

We are going to observe plants and record what we see in drawings and tables.

Resources: Learner's Book, copies of the poster in the Learner's Book. Workbook 1.2 Challenge (optional)

Description: Read the description of the activity in the Learner's Book. Ask the learners to look at the three picture of different plants in the Learner's Book: rice, pond weed and a cactus. Together read the summary of the plants' needs in the table. Ask the learners to tell you about the different plants and where they might live. Ask learners to form groups of three and each person in the group should select a different plant which they will pretend to be.

Give each person two minutes to tell the other about the plant they are going to grow (for example, rice, cactus, pondweed) and the place it would need to live. Ask for two or three learners to share their thoughts about the plant with the class. For example, I want to grow a cactus, I need a hot, dry habitat with lots of Sun. I don't need a lot of rain.

Give the learners a poster like the one in the Learner's Book. Demonstrate how to complete the poster.

Ask learners to complete their posters. By the end of this activity, learners should realise that all living things have needs and they rely on a habitat.

At this point you might ask learners to complete the Workbook 1.2 Challenge, where learners are asked to complete sentences about a seed planted in different habitats.

> **Practical guidance:** If the groups of three cannot agree on who will be which plant, allocate the plants to them yourself.

> **Differentiation ideas:** When the groups of three are formed, you might support less confident learners by placing them in groups with more confident learners.

Challenge more confident learners by asking them to design the perfect habitat for plants.

> **Assessment ideas:** Select three of the tables completed by learners about different plants. Display these to the learners. Can they tell you about the differences between the habitats?

3 Think like a scientist 2: Finding all the plants in a habitat (15–20 minutes)

Learning intention: We are going to describe different plants in a habitat.

We are going to compare different habitats for plants.

We are going to observe plants and record what we see in drawings and tables.

We are going to use a magnifying glass.

Resources: Learner's Book, copies of the record table (2–3 per learner) (you can print 2 or 3 per A4 sheet), a poster-sized copy of the record table,

access to outdoors (if this is impossible, take learners to windows overlooking areas with plants, or display photographs of different habitats with plants, alternatively meet your class at the end of playtime outside and do the activity as you come into school), magnifying glasses, clipboards (optional)

Description: Read the description of the activity in the Learner's Book. Take the learners outside and ask them to observe a plant and complete a record table for that plant. Then ask them to move onto another plant and complete another record sheet. After learners have completed at least two record sheets, return to class. Ask learners to place the records on their table. Then ask everyone to stand and move around the room so that they can read the records of other learners. After returning to the seats, ask learners to re-read their own records. Ask the learners what things the plants need to live, for example, light water, soil and air. Ask if they notice that plants all need these same things.

> **Practical guidance:** While you are observing the plants, look out for plants that are struggling, for example, very small, perhaps with few leaves or yellowing leaves. Ask learners why this plant is not growing well (it may be short of light, water, or good soil). You can accept suggestions such as 'it has been eaten' or 'someone has stepped on it'. Learners should be clear that the habitat is not quite right for this plant.

> **Differentiation ideas:** Observe the learners carefully when they are observing plants and making records. If they appear to lack confidence, support them back in class by pairing them with a more confident learner.

Challenge more confident learners by asking them to think about different-sized plants. Do they need more, or less, Sun, water and shelter?

> **Assessment ideas:** Ask learners to join with a friend and share their records. Ask them to arrange the records on the table in two groups: plants growing in flower beds and plants growing in other places. Can the learners explain that each plant was in a suitable habitat (it could get light, water, soil and air)?

Plenary ideas

1 Making a habitat in our classroom (10–15 minutes)

Resources: Sheets of paper and a pen. Ten pieces of paper with the word plant on them or the names of different plants, for example, mango tree, grass, orchid, fern, etc.

Description: Select a group of ten learners to be plants. Ask them to sit or stand in different places in part of the classroom. Give these learners the pieces of paper with the names of plants on them. Ask some to stand as trees and others to make the shape of a bush or other plant. Explain to the other learners that we are going to make a habitat for these plants. Ask them to talk in pairs to decide what we will need (if needed prompt with light, water soil and air). Now ask learners to suggest what we need to provide. Write each suggestion on one or two pieces of paper and ask learners to place them in the habitat to show what we are giving. For example, ask one child to hold the word Sun high so light can shine on all our plants, ask that the word soil is scattered on the floor, the word water can go on the floor as 'puddles', the word air can be held here and there by learners. Ask the children who are plants to slowly 'grow'. Ask them whether they are happy plants in their new habitat.

⟩ **Reflection ideas:** If plants could choose their own habitat, what would it be like? Where would they live?

2 Growing plants in class (15 minutes)

Resources: A tray, soil, seeds or plants, a jug of water

Description: Ask the learners to look around the classroom and ask, is this room a good habitat for a plant? Does it have light, water, and soil? (The room will have light and water is available, but it is not a habitat for plants.)

Show the learners the tray and other resources ask them to talk in threes about how we could make a small habitat for plants in class.

Ask them to report back. Select two learners to make the habitat and ask other learners to give them step-by-step instructions (put soil in the tray, plant the plant or seeds, water the tray a little).

⟩ **Reflection ideas:** What is an ideal habitat for human beings?

CROSS-CURRICULAR LINKS

This topic links to environmental education because it is about the needs of living things and the way living things rely on the environment.

Homework ideas

Ask learners to 'Find a plant friend at home.' Ask learners to find a plant in the house or garden at home and draw it in its habitat. Ask them to check whether the plant has light, water, soil and air. Can learners make this plant their plant friend who they will look after?

Ask learners to design and draw a nature garden for the school. This is a place with lots of different plants, tall and short, different coloured flowers, big leaves and small leaves, different shaped leaves.

1.3 Animals in different habitats

LEARNING PLAN

Learning objectives	Learning intention	Success criteria
2Be.01 Know that an environment in which a plant or animal naturally lives is its habitat.	• We are going to describe the place an animal lives as its habitat.	• I can describe the place an animal lives as its habitat.

CONTINUED

Learning objectives	Learning intention	Success criteria
2Be.03 Identify similarities and differences between local environments in terms of hot, cold, dry, wet, many plants, few plants, many animals and few animals.	• We are going to compare different habitats for animals.	• I can compare different habitats for animals.
2TWSc.06 Collect and record observations and/or measurements by annotating images and completing simple tables.	• We are going to make observations and record them in drawings.	• I can make observations and record them in drawings.

LANGUAGE SUPPORT

This topic, like this last one, includes comparison of habitats so be prepared to structure discussion around the language of comparison.

For example, use open questions such as: 'What do we see here?' 'What is different here?' 'What is similar?'

When you are talking about the homes of different animals, you can teach words like, hive (bee) and point out that some words for animals' homes, are used for the home of several animals. For example, a nest is the home for a bird and an ant.

Support general language development and learners for who English is a second language by:

• making the learning of animal names a fun activity, for example, this animal slides on the ground, its tongue is forked, its a … (snake),

• asking learners to repeat words to you in different voices, you demonstrate the word in the voice and they repeat it back in the same voice, for example, say insect as a mouse would say it in a squeaky voice, learners repeat it back to you; now say insect as a giant would say it and they repeat it back to you in that voice, other options are to say it as a frog, a superhero, a robot,

• add to a class poster of environmental words.

attract: get interest so that something is drawn to it

clues: things we observe which help us understand

droppings: solid waste made by animals

egg: a shell or case made by female animals, each contains young

hide: keeping out of sight

insect: a small animal with three body parts and six legs

scare: frighten

table: a grid of squares we use to write or draw results

tracks: marks made by an animal as it moves

Common misconceptions

Misconception	How to identify	How to overcome
Some learners may think that animals can live anywhere or in many habitats.	Ask learners to draw or talk about the places animals can live.	Refer to some animals that have very specific needs, for example, dugong (lives in unpolluted warm shallow water with lots of underwater plants, mainly seagrass). Then to animals that are more flexible but still have needs, for example, a pigeon.

Starter ideas

1 Animals can hide (15 minutes)

Resources: An example of camouflage fabric or clothing, for example, a green jacket to wear in a forest

Description: Explain that some animals can be eaten by bigger animals so they will try to hide. To help this some animals have skin, fur or feathers that blend with their habitat. Ask the learners to talk with a partner and then report to the class about any animals they know are camouflaged, for example, artic fox, snowy owl, yellow lizards living on sand. Explain that sometimes people wear camouflage clothing so they can hide. Ask a learner to come out, ask them to pretend to take a photograph. Ask the learners what colour of clothing would camouflage this learner if they wanted to take photographs of, or film, animals in a snowy place? Repeat this question format about filming animals in a forest environment, filming lizards in a desert environment or filming bats in a cave environment. Ask what would happen to an animal if it lived in the wrong habitat, for example, a yellow lizard living on black sand or soil (it would easily be seen an eaten). After this activity, learners should understand that animals use camouflage to hide from other animals. This camouflage is suited to the habitat they live in.

Learners may look at animals around them as friendly and all safe. Encourage them to realise that some are eaten by others, this is natural but affects the way animals live, for example, hiding.

2 Different habitat sizes (15 minutes)

Resources: Learner's Book, Workbook 1.3 Focus (optional)

Description: You might start this activity with the Workbook 1.3 Focus activity which asks learners to link animals with possible habitats. Ask learners to look at the eagle in the picture at the start of this unit. Ask learners about the eagle's habitat, what is the habitat like, what food is the eagle looking for (small animals for example, rats, mice, frogs). Ask how big is the eagle's habitat. (It is very big, (many kilometres) if you walked all day in the mountains you would walk across the habitat.) Ask about a mouse. The eagle hunts for animals like mice. How big is a mouse's habitat? (it is smaller, perhaps part of a hillside as big as a soccer field, or smaller), what food is a mouse looking for (seeds). Ask the learners to talk about other animals that have either a very large habitat (for example, any large carnivore or whale) or a small habitat (for example, any ground-based insect like an ant, invertebrate or small reptile or mammal). Learners may have a limited idea of a habitat, for example, a woodland or park. Can they talk about different habitats in an area?

Main teaching ideas

1 Think like a scientist: Habitats for animals around school (30–40 minutes)

Learning intention: We are going to describe the place an animal lives as its habitat.

We are going to compare different habitats for animals.

We are going to make observations and record them in drawings.

Resources: Learner's Book, access to an outdoor area and a spade and tray (if this is not possible access to a window which overlooks an outdoor area (open the window so that you might hear bird song – a clue to animals around) or to photographs taken in an outdoor area, trays of soil, lolly sticks and magnifying glasses, copies of the recording table from the Learner's Book, clipboards, white paper, Workbook 1.3 Practice (optional)

Description: You might start this activity by asking learners to complete the Workbook 1.3 Practice exercise, which asks learners to complete sentences about different habitats of several animals. Read the description of the activity in the Learner's Book and take learners to observe habitats in the school grounds if possible. In this activity it is important to talk with learners about the habitat and the places it offers for animals to live (any plants to eat or hide in, rocks or leaves to hide in, dead leaves to eat). You are likely to hear birdsong and more likely to see insects and other very small animals. Make sure you observe at least two different habitats so that you can compare them. For example, do they provide places to shelter or plants to eat? Are they damp or dry or hot or cool?

If you are outdoors, use a spade to observe one habitat. For example, gently lift larger rocks or leaves so that learners can look to see what is underneath (explain that you will put the rock and leaves back as they may be home to animals). You might observe soil as a different habitat by using a spade to dig a small hole, placing the soil you have dug out onto a tray or large sheet of white paper. Learners may be able to observe insects and small animals in the soil.

Also ask learners to look out for clues about animals living in the habitat, for example, birdsong, flying insects, leaves that have been eaten, animal droppings (for example, bird lime). Explain that as scientists observing, learners should use eyes and ears. Ask learners now to complete the tables to record what they have observed.

If possible, bring trays of soil into the classroom and allow learners to gently move the soil with a stick and observe, ideally with a magnifying glass. By the end of this activity, learners should be clear that they can learn about habitats, but they may have to look carefully and think about what they see.

> **Practical guidance:** Ask learners to be very gentle with small animals. Make sure everyone washes their hands with soap and water after the lesson.

> **Differentiation ideas:** Support less confident learners with prompts such as these. Can you see any leaves that have been eaten? Can you hear any animals?

Challenge more confident learners by asking them to describe the different habitats they have seen, for example, under a rock, on the bark of a tree, the tree leaves, the soil at the base of a shrub or tree.

> **Assessment ideas:** Ask learners to talk about two different habitats and the living things they might find there, for example, part of a wall and another one which is larger for example, a tree.

2 Activity 1: A habitat for snails (20–30 minutes)

Learning intention: We are going to describe the place an animal lives as its habitat.

Resources: Learner's Book, snails, soil, leaves, twigs, small rocks, water, plastic fish tank and lid

Description: Ask learners about the kind of habitat a snail would need given that it needs food, water, shelter and air. Learners may talk about darkness, wet, damp, leaves, twigs, soil and more. Emphasise that snails like damp conditions but not very wet.

Ask learners to talk in pairs about the way we might design a suitable habitat for snails using a plastic fish tank. Ask them in pairs to draw their ideas, some of which can then be shared with the class before setting up the fish tank for the snails. Emphasise the need for some dampness, leaves and a little wood, soil and rocks to provide places to shelter and hide. If the soil or leaves are very dry, ask a learner to add a little water.

> **Practical guidance:** If you cannot find three or four snails, then slugs or woodlice will do because they like similar conditions. You will need another container with a lid for the snails/ invertebrates before the habitat is ready. If learners are concerned about the lid preventing the animals getting enough air, explain that these small animals use very little air and that there is more than enough in the tank.

Remind learners that they must wash their hands with soap and water after handling, soil, leaves, twigs or snails

> **Differentiation ideas:** Ask confident learners about why the snails like to hide. This is because they might be eaten by animals including birds. Can

they say more about the kind of habitats snails will therefore like?

> **Assessment ideas:** Ask learners to prepare a very short text message (as might be sent on a mobile phone) which starts. 'I have made good habitat for snails that has…'

3 Activity 2: Let's make an insect hotel (20–30 minutes)

Learning intention: We are going to describe the place an animal lives as its habitat.

We are going to make observations and record them in drawings.

Resources: Learner's Book, short sticks (10–15 cm), dried grassy stems, short bamboo canes (10–15 cm) or sticks, string or thin wire (keep the sharp ends of wire away from eyes), scissors, Workbook 1.3 Challenge (optional)

Description: Read the description of the activity in the Learner's Book. Demonstrate how to hold a bundle of sticks or canes while another person ties string around and a string to hang the insect 'hotel'. Ask the learners to talk in pairs about why we call this an insect hotel (a place to rest and hide, the stick, can also be eaten by some animals, a place to lay eggs). Ask them to report back their ideas.

Ask learners to photograph or draw their insect hotels and to draw insects (for example, beetles) living there. Label it to show the spaces in which a small animal could hide. Explain that this will be an important part of the habitat because it is a shelter and that insect needs to go out walking and flying looking for more food.

Ask why it is that, when there are lots on insects in a habitat, we tend to find lots of birds around (many birds eat insects).

If possible, take the learners outside to hang their insect 'hotels' in bushes and trees. If space is limited, wind string around several 'hotels' to make a big 'hotel' and tie this into the bush or tree. The 'hotels' can also be laid on the ground with soil or a stone half covering them. Conclude by making sure that learners understand that all animals need a habitat and within it somewhere to rest or hide.

You might conclude this activity with Workbook 1.3 Challenge which asks learners to complete sentences about habitats and to identify the needs of animals and of plants.

> **Practical guidance:** Make sure that learners wash their hands thoroughly after this activity.

> **Differentiation ideas:** If learners have a lot of difficulty tying the string around the stick bundles, assist them with sticky tape or a rubber band around the bundle while that tie the string.

> **Assessment ideas:** Ask learners to show you where the animals might hide in the bundle and explain why that need a place to shelter.

Plenary ideas

1 Animals' homes (10 minutes)

Resources: Five pieces of paper with the name of an animal on each, for example, bee, bear, bird, rabbit, ant, spider, placed in an envelope

Description: Explain that we are going to play a game. As the learners know, an important part of an animal's habitat is its home. In the envelope are the names of animals. You are going to ask learners to draw out one piece of paper from the envelope, read the animal's name and then ask the class the name of its home. (A bee's home is a hive, bear's a den, a bird's home is a nest, a rabbit's home is a burrow, hole or hutch, an ant lives in a nest, a spider lives in a web.) In each case, ask another learner to describe this home. For example, what is it made of? Where would we find it?

2 Animal footprints (10 minutes)

Resources: A child's foot – with permission, ask if a learner could remove a shoe (they can leave on a sock) so that you can draw around it, drawn copies of other animals footprints

Description: Explain that scientists studying animals often have to look for clues. One clue can be footprints. Show the class the human footprint which they should all recognise. Ask them what would it tell us if we found these footprints on a sandy beach (it tells us that someone has been there before us). Now play a game. Show the class an animal's footprint and ask them what the animal is. Ask them to explain why they think it is that animal. Repeat this for other footprints.

For information

Cat   Dog   Wolf   Raccoon

Monkey   Bear   Rabbit   Tiger

Chicken   Dove   Duck   Pig

Cow   Horse   Elephant   Crocodile

> **Reflection ideas:** What signs do we humans leave around which would give clues to where we have been? (The police often look for fingerprints – learners may have seen this on TV.)

CROSS-CURRICULAR LINKS

This topic links to environmental education and to geography because it is about places in, and features of, the local environment and the animals that live there. It shows learners that the environment is very important to animals and that we should care for these animals.

Homework ideas

Ask learners to talk to people at home about wild animals that have been seen locally including insects and birds.

Having made an insect hotel at school, ask learners help insects with a home near their home. Ask them to make an insect hotel at home to be left in bush in a garden or park.

1.4 Rocks and the environment

LEARNING PLAN

Learning objectives	Learning intention	Success criteria
2ESp.01 Describe and compare different types of rock.	• We are going to describe and compare different rocks.	• I can describe and compare different rocks.
2ESp.02 Know rocks are extracted from the Earth in different ways, including from quarries, mines and riverbeds. **2ESp.03** Know that human activity can affect the environment.	• We are going to find how rocks are dug up and how this affects the environment.	• I can talk about how rocks are dug up and how this affects the environment.
2TWSp.02 Make predictions about what they think will happen. **2TWSa.01** Describe what happened during an enquiry and if it matched their predictions	• We are going to make predictions and see if they are right.	• I can make predictions and see if they are right.

CONTINUED

Learning objectives	Learning intention	Success criteria
2TWSc.01 Sort and group objects, materials and living things based on observations of the similarities and differences between them.	• We are going to sort rocks using water.	• I can sort rocks using water.
2TWSc.02 Use given equipment appropriately.	• We are going to use equipment safely.	• I can use equipment safely.
2TWSc.06 Collect and record observations and/or measurements by annotating images and completing simple tables.	• We are going to make and record observations in pictures and tables.	• I can make and record observations in pictures and tables.

LANGUAGE SUPPORT

The topic of rocks is perhaps one where learners are less familiar with the words, for example, quarry and gravel. The activities present many opportunities for learners to speak and listen. This is important for all learners, but particularly any who find language in general, or English in particular, a challenge.

- As you begin this topic, ask learners to make their first page of notes a glossary (a page where they add new words with a definition or picture).
- Use Activity 1 to develop a display of rocks, or photographs of rocks, with lots of associated language because this will help learners become familiar with the language and ideas.
- Make audio recordings of learners, or yourself, talking about rocks. Play these back to learners so that they have the opportunity to hear the language of the topic repeatedly in context.

- Introduce a puppet or toy as an individual the learners can teach about rocks. Ask them to explain things to the puppet. For example, what is a quarry?

absorb: when water soaks into the material

explosive: a material that will blow things apart

gravel: small pieces of rock

mine: hole dug to extract rocks or minerals

quarry: a place where the surface rocks are removed so that rock from just below the surface can be dug out

rock: a hard material that comes from the Earth's surface sample

sample: a piece of a material

stones: small rocks

swirl: make a liquid spin

waterproof: a material that does not let water through.

Common misconceptions

Misconception	How to identify	How to overcome
Many learners may consider rocks to be very large heavy objects.	When learners handle small rock samples, or sand, they may be reluctant to call it rock.	When giving examples of rocks, try to give examples of all sizes of rock. Be clear that sand is made of pieces of rock.
Learners may think that brick and concrete are rocks. They may contain stones, but these materials have been made by people.	When observing in the local environment or school building, learners may refer to bricks and concrete as rocks.	Point out that bricks and concrete are made by people. You would not normally find these in a natural place unless put there by people. Learners may recall seeing bricks and concrete being used on a building site.

Starter ideas

1 How do we dig up rocks? (5 minutes)

Resources: Pictures of a quarry, mine and river bed

Description: Show learners pictures of a quarry, mine and river bed. Check that learners can tell you what is happening in each picture. Explain that these are the main ways that people get rock. Some of this work is very dangerous, deep underground or in quarries where people use tools, machines and even explosives to break up the rock so that it can be put in wagons and trucks and moved to places it is needed. You might refer to any mines or quarries that may be nearby. Explain that quarries, mines and rivers are dangerous places and learners should never play near them. Ask learners about rocks used to build local roads and buildings, and ask where the rock comes from (from mines, quarries or river beds).

2 What do we make from rock? (10–15 minutes)

Resources: a rock or stone, talcum powder or a stick of chalk

Description: Look at the pictures in this topic which show a stone bridge and a stone fountain. Can learners think of other things we use rock to make (roofing, buildings, paths, roads, walls, jewellery, fire). Can learners think of ways we use rock to improve the environment? (To make new ponds and lakes, to make nature reserves, to build homes for animals). Can learners see how rock has been used to make their life better? (roads, hospitals, schools, houses, airports, dams etc).

Learners may not be aware of the use of rocks to make so many things we need.

Main teaching ideas

1 Think like a scientist 1: Learning more about rocks (30–40 minutes)

Learning intention: We are going to describe and compare different rocks.

We are going to find how rocks are dug up and how this affects the environment.

We are going to make observations and record them in pictures and tables.

We are going to use equipment safely.

Resources: Learner's Book, rock samples, magnifying glasses, paper clips, rock samples (a range of four to six different rocks, if possible provide a set for each group of four to six learners), record sheets similar to the one in the Learner's Book, Workbook 1.4 Focus (optional) Digital Classroom video: How do we dig up rocks? (optional); Digital Classroom Science investigators video: What are rocks used for? (optional)

Description: Read the description of the activity in the Learner's Book.

> **Digital Classroom:** If you have access to the Digital Classroom component, use the video 'How do we dig up rocks?' to show learners some examples of different rocks and rock extraction. The i button will explain how to use the video. Discuss what they observe.

Give learners a few minutes to handle and observe the rock samples (if you cannot name them, label them, 1, 2, 3,… etc) using magnifying glasses.

Explain that scientists who study rocks always describe them carefully. Show them the record sheet headings and assist with a word bank of descriptive words. For example, grey, red, white, dull, shiny, hard soft, bits we can see, small bits, no bits we can see, rough, smooth.

Explain that learners can observe with their fingers and eyes and that they can use a magnifying glass to see details that are hard to see with the eye. (Teach learners to hold the rock sample and their own head still while they move the magnifying glass towards the sample and back to focus a clear view.)

It will help at this point to ask learners to complete Workbook 1.4 Focus which illustrates different rocks, their names and uses.

Demonstrate the hardness test by trying to scratch the rock with the paper clip (soft rock like chalk will be easy to scratch and even break off little pieces, harder rock like granite may be impossible to scratch).

Ideally give each table or group one or two samples to test. Ask them to observe and test all the rocks and to record their observations on the table.

When it comes to the uses of rocks, it will help if you make up a poster for this. Ask learners to think about each rock in turn and suggest uses. You might draw their attention to the Learner's Book which offers some ideas. Prompt learners with suggestions such as:

> limestone: we use it to build walls, buildings
>
> coal: we use it to burn to keep us warm
>
> chalk: we use it to write on a black board
>
> granite: we use it for building and floor tiles
>
> marble: we use it for floor tiles and carving
>
> sandstone: we use it for building.

> **Digital Classroom:** If you have access to the Digital Classroom component, use the Science investigators video 'What are rocks used for?' to show learners some examples of what rocks are used for. The i button will explain how to use the video.

When learners have finished several record tables, use some to create a display of the rock samples and information tables. By the end of this activity, learners should be able to see that scientists can gather information by observing things and that rocks are interesting in lots of ways.

> **Practical guidance:** Safety – when learners are scratching rocks warn them to take care.

Learners should avoid breathing in any rock dust.

> **Differentiation ideas:** Ensure that the less confident learners can see key words on posters you have made.

Challenge more confident learners by asking them to write a plan for test of hardness of three or four different rocks (they can use the test using a paper clip mentioned above).

> **Assessment ideas:** You could mix up the rock sample reports and ask learners to read one record table and select the appropriate rock sample.

2   Think like a scientist 2: Does this rock absorb water? (20 minutes)

Learning intention: We are going to describe and compare different rocks.

We are going to make predictions and compare these to our results.

We are going to sort rocks using water.

We are going to make observations and record them in pictures and tables.

Resources: Learner's Book, teaspoon, three to five different rock samples per pair or small group, small pots of water, magnifying glasses, copies of the record table similar to the one in the Learner's Book, scrap paper (newspaper) to catch drips

Description: Read the description of the activity in the Learner's Book. Provide the learners with rock samples. These can be named but, if not, they can be numbered or described, for example, the white rock, the grey rock etc. Explain that in this lesson we will use two important words, absorb and waterproof. Explain that absorb means that water soaks into the material for example, like a paper tissue. Waterproof means the water runs off like it runs off plastic. Ask the learners to predict if they think the rocks will absorb water or are waterproof. This can be one prediction for all the rocks or, better, ask them to make a prediction for each one. Record these on a poster. Record it like this.

Our question – Do these rocks absorb water or are they waterproof?

Prediction – Our prediction is …

Now ask learners, working in pairs, to carefully and very slowly drop four drops of water on a rock and then observe whether the water is absorbed or runs off (waterproof). Ask learners to share their results and record the results on the record table. Ask learners to compare the result to their prediction.

Ask the learners to repeat the test with another rock sample.

After learners have tested and recorded results from around four samples, ask them to describe their findings to another pair. By the end of this activity, learners should realise that this is another way we can talk about and test different rocks.

> **Practical guidance:** Some learners might confuse the rock being wet and the rock absorbing water. You might allow them to wet a paper tissue or newspaper to see what we mean by absorb.

> **Differentiation ideas:** Some less confident learners may benefit from step-by-step instruction and support. Try at all times to let them work without your help. You might pair less confident learners with more confident learners.

Challenge more confident learners by giving them a bigger range of rocks to test.

> **Assessment ideas:** Ask learners to place the rocks that they have observed in order, starting with the one which absorbed least water and working to the one which absorbed the most.

3 Think like a scientist 3: Sorting stones with water (20 minutes)

Learning intention: We are going to describe and compare different rocks.

We are going to find how rocks are dug up and how this affects the environment.

We are going to sort rocks using water

We are going to make predictions about what we think will happen.

Resources: Learner's Book, soil with stones in or added, or an alternative is a mixture of sand, gravel and stones, water, bowls, buckets or trays, newspaper or larger trays to protect the tables, hand towels, Workbook 1.4 Practice (optional), Digital Classroom video: How do we dig up rocks? (optional)

Description: Read the description of the activity in the Learner's Book. Explain that we dig some rocks out of the ground but we also get a lot of rock from rivers.

> **Digital Classroom:** If you have access to the Digital Classroom component, you could use the video from Think like a scientist 1: 'How do we dig up rocks?' to show learners some examples of different rocks and rock extraction. The i button will explain how to use the video.

You might ask learners to complete the Workbook 1.4 Practice exercise, which asks learners to complete sentences about rock extraction.

Explain that people have, for a very long time, used water to sort rocks and stone, especially sand and small stones. Some people even use this method to find gold in streams in some places in the world! Ask a learner to demonstrate placing the soil mix or stone mix in a tray, adding water and gently rocking/rotating the tray so that water moves too and fro and slowly the different sized pieces settle out. (You might ask if any learners have visited a stream or river and seen how sandy or gravel beaches lie at the sides. Explain that the tray is the same thing but smaller.)

Now ask learners in pairs or threes to set up the equipment and have a go at sorting or 'panning' the pieces of rock with the water.

After everyone has had a go, ask the learners to report back what happened, how long it took and the result. The water should have sorted the particles according to rock particle size, smaller particles together and larger ones together. Explain that moving water does this in rivers and at the seaside all the time, and that this is how we get sandy beaches.

> **Practical guidance:** Ensure that all learners wash their hands with soap and water after this activity. Explain that stones look clean but that they have not been washed and so may have germs on them.

> **Differentiation ideas:** Support less confident learners by pairing them with confident learners.

Challenge more confident learners by asking them to predict what might happen.

> **Assessment ideas:** Ask learners what would happen to even larger stones in the mix. (They would be heavy and stay together, they would be sorted just like the other pieces.)

Plenary ideas

1 Chocolate rocks (15 minutes)

Resources: Different types of chocolate, for example, white chocolate, chocolate with fruit in, chocolate with nuts in, chocolate with biscuit bits in, chocolate with a soft toffee, dark chocolate, light coloured chocolate.

Description:

Safety: Check that learners are not allergic to chocolate or nuts.

Explain that the chocolates you have brought to school are all very different and, like rocks, are different colours and some have different 'bits' in them. Break the chocolate so that the learners can observe the bits of chocolate as if they were rocks. Explain that we can group the chocolate bits. Ask the learners to group dark chocolates together and light chocolate in another group. As an alternative, ask learners to group smooth chocolate together separate from a group of chocolate with bits in. Can the learners suggest any other ways to divide the chocolates into two groups?

Safety: After handling, this chocolate cannot be eaten (also sweets are a treat as they can be bad for health).

> Reflection ideas: Ask learners, when you are learning science, does it help you to have fun? How does this help?

2 Are quarries good or bad? (10–15 minutes)

Resources: Workbook 1.4 Challenge (optional)

Description: We need rocks for so many things, so quarries are essential, but quarries can destroy habitats.

Ask learners, now that they have learned about quarries, can they explain how new quarry might affect a local environment, for example, trees chopped down, plants killed, animals lose their homes, water polluted? Are there ways that the quarry workers might help living things? Share learners' ideas, for example, planting new trees, making a nature reserve, stopping pollution.

Explain that this is an example of how people can damage the environment but, if they think about it, can help to.

Learners might complete the Workbook 1.4 Challenge which illustrates and asks for sentences to be completed about the effect of quarrying on an environment.

> Reflection ideas: Ask learners these questions. Does science help you to look at the world in a different way? Can you see ideas that help all living things?

> CROSS-CURRICULAR LINKS

This topic links strongly with geography because it is about rocks and where and how they are dug from the ground.

Homework ideas

Ask learners to ask family members about rocks at home used in the floor, steps, walls, paths. Can learners list or draw where rocks are used?

On the walk home, or from home to school, can learners observe different rocks used in walls, paths, buildings, statues, roads. What colours do they see?

1.5 How can we care for our environment?

> LEARNING PLAN

Learning objectives	Learning intention	Success criteria
2ESp.03 Know that human activity can affect the environment.	• We will find out about how people can change the environment.	• I can find out about how people can change the environment.

CONTINUED

Learning objectives	Learning intention	Success criteria
1TWSc.06 Collect and record observations and/or measurements by annotating images and completing simple tables.	• We are going to make observations and record them in pictures and tables.	• I can make and record my observation with drawing and tables.
2TWSp.02 Make predictions about what they think will happen. **2TWSa.01** Describe what happened during an enquiry and if it matched their predictions	• We will make predictions and see if they are right.	• I can make predictions and see if they are right.

LANGUAGE SUPPORT

The environment is a word and an idea that learners may have heard of, and may be very keen to find out about, for example, the effect of pollution on sealife. Support your learners' language in the following ways:

• if the environment features in the news, draw your learners' attention to it,

• look for opportunities to develop this language about the environment in other lessons, for example, in English, you might talk or write about an animal living in a polluted world, or write letters to local organisations asking about ways they prevent damage to the environment,

• ask learners to bring books or information from home about animals and the environment, use these to raise interest in the language of environmental protection for example, recycling.

litter: something dropped on the ground which should be put in a bin

material: a substance used to make something

nature reserve: a place which is made to be a good habitat for plants and animals

protect: to take care of something or someone

recycle: reuse a material so that it does not get dumped

Common misconceptions

Misconception	How to identify	How to overcome
Some learners may think that as they are so young and only one person, they cannot have a good effect on the environment.	You may notice that they don't appear to suggest anything they could do to help the environment.	Explain that we all have to help. If everyone in the class or school does not drop litter, that is 30 people or even 200 people. This soon has a big effect.

Starter ideas

1   Rubbish on a beach (10–15 minutes)

Resources: Learner's Book, Workbook 1.5 Focus

Description: Ask learners to look at the picture of the beach in the Learner's Book.
Ask them to talk in twos or threes about what they see and what effect this will have on animals and plants (many would be killed for example, poisoned, choked, tangled up and drowned). Remind learners about the many good things we do in the environment e.g. planting parks.

Ask learners where the litter and rubbish comes from (from people). Ask them how this could be stopped (by people using litter bins). Ask them if it is important (animals help to keep the environment healthy – for example, some animals eat dead animals).

At this point you might ask learners to complete Workbook 1.5 Focus where children talk about a damaged environment.

2   Recycling (10 minutes)

Resources: Workbook 1.5 Practice

Description: Ask if learners have seen plastic litter in the area or in places they have visited. Do they know that we can reuse plastic litter? It can be made into useful things like plastic rulers. Have they heard this called recycling? Do they or people they know recycle any materials, for example, plastic, paper, metal? Ask learners to talk in pairs and then report back to the class on the harm that plastic can do to the environment. For example, plastic gets broken and animals eat and are poisoned by small pieces of plastic, plastic bags can choke or suffocate land and sea animals. Ask learners if they know where they can recycle materials. Do learners realise that they can have a big effect? (If they avoid dropping one piece of litter each day, that is many hundreds over their time at this school.)

You might ask learners to complete Workbook 1.5 Practice, where learners are asked answer questions about recycling symbols and recycling by a class of learners.

Ask learners how they can reduce plastic waste (avoid single use plastic bottles and bags, re use plastic when you can for example, cups, always recycle plastic or put it in a bin).

Main teaching ideas

1   Activity 1: Litter (30–40 minutes)

Learning intention: We will find out about how people can change the environment.

Resources: Learner's Book, opportunity to look outside at the school site or beyond, (if this is difficult, learners could look out of windows or look at local photographs, alternatively meet them at the end of playtime outside and do the activity as you come into school), poster paper

Worksheet 1.5A, 1.5B or 1.5C (optional).

Description: Read the description of the activity in the Learner's Book.

Take the learners to look at different areas around the school. Can they see evidence that people have had a good affect on the environment? For example, paths, roads, gardens, litter bins. Can they see signs that people have not cared for the environment? For example, litter, plants which are damaged, broken items.

Back in class, talk about the things you have seen and know about in the area around school. Can the learners talk about ways they could help the environment, for example, think of ways to reduce litter or ways to recycle things or places they might sow seeds? Ask the learners, in pairs, to sketch their ideas onto a poster (at least one or two ideas depending on time you have). For example, providing more litter bins, putting up signs for example, 'care for our trees', having a litter patrol, etc. Then ask several pairs to report their ideas back to the class.

> **Practical guidance:** Take care picking up litter. Learners should only pick up litter if they are wearing protective gloves or using a litter picker.

> **Differentiation ideas:** You might ask learners to complete Worksheets 1.5A, 1.5B or 1.5C. These provide a picture of an environment. In Worksheet 1.5A learners circle environmental problems, in Worksheet 1.5B learners complete sentences about ways to improve the environment and in Worksheet 1.5C learners link an explanation to the problem in the picture.

> **Assessment ideas:** Ask learners to write an environment quiz. Learners have to ask the questions (to which they know the answer). For example, what should we do with litter?

2 Activity 2: Making a nature reserve (20–30 minutes)

Learning intention: We will find out about how people can change the environment.

Resources: Learner's Book

Description: Read the description of the activity in the Learner's Book. Explain that we can affect the environment in many ways. Ask the learners to talk in pairs about the picture in the Learner's Book. What can they see? What is happening? Ask learners in pairs to write or draw ideas they might suggest to the children in the picture. Ask learners to report ideas back while you record these on a board or poster. Be willing to prompt learners with questions. For example, can we provide water for animals? Can we help to have more plants? Which plants attract insects? Could we help with places for animals to live, for example, insect hotels, or a pile of rocks or logs, or a wet area? Could we remove litter? Could we improve the soil or plant a tree?

At the end of the activity, make sure that learners can see steps they could take to improve the environment for living things.

Learners might complete Workbook 1.5 Focus where they have to decide which of four statements are right about environmental damage.

⟩ **Practical guidance:** If you decide to use these ideas to make a nature reserve at school, talk to the site manager about your plans and the importance of this project for the education of the learners.

⟩ **Differentiation ideas:** Have less confident learners drawing rather than writing. Display key words on a mini poster for them.

Challenge more confident learners by asking them to provide a home for insects, animals that live in water, and birds.

⟩ **Assessment ideas:** Can learners redraw the corner of the school grounds shown in the Learner's Book, adding their own ideas that would help living things?

3 Think like a scientist 1: Survey the environment (20–30 minutes)

Learning intention: We will find out about how people can change the environment.

We are going to make observations and record them in pictures and tables.

We will make predictions and see if they are right.

Resources: Learner's Book, take the learners outside or meet them on the playground after playtime (if this is impossible observe the site from school windows or look at photographs of the area), camera, copies of table from this activity in the Learner's Book, Workbook 1.5 Challenge

Description: Read the description of the activity in the Learner's Book. Explain that before people make changes to the environment they will often survey the area first. Take learners to particular places on the school site where they may observe litter, bins, vehicles, recycling bins. If learners have previously visited these areas, ask them to predict what they might see. Ask them all to study one area or assign groups to look at different areas. Ask learners to complete a record table like the one in the Learner's Book. If possible, allow learners to take digital photographs of areas.

Back in the classroom, discuss the area/s you visited. Was there evidence that people care for the environment? Are there signs that people are not caring for the environment? Can learners suggest ways that we can look after the environment?

By the end of this activity, learners should see how people can affect the enviroment in different ways.

At this point, you might ask learners to complete Workbook 1.5 Challenge, which asks about the effects on the number of animals in a forest that is being chopped down.

⟩ **Practical guidance:** Plan the places you will visit outdoors. Try to include suitable places that the children will have visited previously. As with all outdoor visits, learners must be supervised at all times. Learners must wash their hands after this activity.

⟩ **Differentiation ideas:** Less confident learners may work best in groups including learners who are more confident.

Challenge more confident learners by asking them to survey more than one area.

⟩ **Assessment ideas:** Can the learners tell you about a way they could improve the local environment to help both animals and plants?

Plenary ideas

1   Environment poster (15 minutes)

Description: Ask learners about a caption for a poster which could help other learners around school to care for the environment. Ask them in pairs to think of a message that would remind other learners to take care, for example, Recycle materials, Put litter in the bin; Don't damage the plants; Care for your world; Put water out for the birds, etc.

Ask learners to feed back. Remind them that just talking to friends and family about caring for the environment will help friends and family to make good choices.

> **Reflection ideas:** Ask learners this question. Does learning about the environment help you to help care for the environment in better ways?

2   Environmental hero (10 minutes)

Description: Tell the class about an environmental hero for example, Rachel Carson. Rachel was a scientist who showed the world that chemicals used by farmers could kill wild animals. Now farmers use fewer dangerous chemicals and this has saved many animals. Ask learners whether you have a learner who could be an environment hero. Do you know a learner who tries hard to help the environment? Could you have a certificate for such a person, or would it be for a class of children? How would this help everyone to think about the environment more often?

> **Reflection ideas:** Ask learners if it helps their learning to know about people who have been heroes for the environment. How does it help them as learners/ young people?

CROSS-CURRICULAR LINKS

This topic is strongly linked to geography and environmental education because it helps us learn about our local environment, and ways to help the environment.

Homework ideas

Ask learners to look at home for any recycling that the family do. Are there ways that the family could recycle more things?

Ask learners to listen to the news. Are there any stories about the environment? Are people trying to help the environment? Are people causing a problem?

Topic worksheets

Worksheets 1.5A, 1.5B and 1.5C

These worksheets provide a picture of an environment.

In Worksheet 1.5A learners circle environmental problems.

In Worksheet 1.5B learners complete sentences about ways to improve the environment.

In Worksheet 1.5C learners link an explanation to the problem in the picture.

PROJECT: OUR SCHOOL'S OUTDOOR ENVIRONMENT

2SIC.04 Talk about how science helps us understand our effect on the world around us.

This project can be carried out individually by learners, or in pairs or threes. It is hoped that they would draw on the topics in this unit to form an increasingly detailed picture of the environment of the school and the habitats. You could ask learners initially to write a possible contents page for the project. Ask several learners to present their content pages to share ideas around.

Project: Our school's outdoor environment

Project: Our school's outdoor environment

Make a small book about the environment of the school grounds.

Think about:

- habitats for plants
- habitats for animals
- where you could put an insect hotel
- ways to improve the outdoor school environment for plants and animals
- where you could put a nature reserve.

Use photographs, pictures and words to tell readers about the school grounds and the animals and plants that live there now.

Make sure you show some good habitats for animals and plants. Think of ways to improve habitats or make new ones.

How would you care for and improve the outdoor spaces around the school?

33 ›

⟩2 Forces and movement

Unit plan

Topic	Approximate number of learning hours	Outline of learning content	Resources
2.1 Forces around us	2	Identifying forces as pushes and pulls that can move or stop things. Comparing the size of pushes using paper rockets.	**Learner's Book:** Activity: Using forces to move things and stop things Think like a scientist: Make a paper rocket launcher **Workbook:** Topic 2.1 **Digital Classroom:** Activity – Push or pull?
2.2 Changing shape	4	Investigating how forces change the shape of some objects. Measuring with non-standard units and looking for simple number patterns in the results.	**Learner's Book:** Think like a scientist 1: Finding patterns in results Think like a scientist 2: How forces can change rubber bands **Workbook:** Topic 2.2 **Teacher's Resource:** ⬇ Worksheets: 2.2A, 2.2B, 2.2C **Digital Classroom:** Activity – Measuring height
2.3 Changing speed	3	Asking scientific questions about speed and talking about how to find out the answers. Investigating speed by making balls speed up and slow down.	**Learner's Book:** Think like a scientist 1: Asking questions about speed Think like a scientist 2: Blow the ball **Workbook:** Topic 2.3 **Digital Classroom:** Song – That's a force

Topic	Approximate number of learning hours	Outline of learning content	Resources
2.4 Changing direction	2	Observing the forces that make us change direction when moving. Investigating and making predictions about how forces make moving balls change direction.	**Learner's Book:** Activity: Feel the force Think like a scientist: This way or that way? **Workbook:** Topic 2.4 **Teacher's Resource:** ⬇ Worksheets: 2.4A, 2.4B, 2.4C **Digital Classroom:** Science investigators video – How can we change the movement of a ball?

Across unit resources

Learner's Book:

Project: How people use forces

Check your progress quiz

Teacher's Resource:

⬇ Language worksheets 1 and 2

⬇ Diagnostic check

Digital Classroom:

⬇ End-of-unit quiz

BACKGROUND KNOWLEDGE

Forces can speed things up, slow things down or make things change direction or change shape. The size of the force is important. A person pushing on a huge rock will not be able to make it move. This is because the force of gravity, pulling down on the rock, is much greater than the force of the person pushing it.

If two people pull with the same strength in opposite directions on a rope, the rope will not move. This is because the forces are balanced. If one of the people pulls with a larger force than the other, the rope will begin

to move towards that person. The forces are now unbalanced and the direction of movement is the same as the direction of the larger force.

Most materials will change shape if a strong enough force is applied. Some materials, such as a rubber band, will return to their original shape after the force is removed. These materials are known as elastic materials. Most elastic materials will break if too much force is applied.

When there is a change in speed or direction of a moving object, there is always a force at work.

CONTINUED

Many people think that if a moving object, such as a rolling ball, stops this is because there is no force to keep it moving. In fact, the ball stops because of the force of friction which slows it down. Without friction to slow it down and with no other forces acting on it, the ball would continue moving in a straight line at the same speed. This never happens on Earth because of the forces of friction, air resistance and gravity.

When you push a moveable object away from you it will move away from you. However,

if an object is making itself move, then the movement will be in the opposite direction to the push. For example, to make a skateboard move forwards you have to push backwards, a propeller pushes water backwards to move a boat forward.

Weight, friction, magnetism, air resistance and up-thrust are all different types of force, but they are all pushes or pulls. For example, your weight pulls you down towards the ground, and magnets can pull together or push apart.

TEACHING SKILLS FOCUS

Active learning

Ask learners to recognize forces

When you are teaching about push and pull forces, always look for an example of a larger push or pull, for example, for example, pull and push a door open, and then a smaller push or pull, for example for example, pull or push a paper clip. Where possible, allow learners to physically experience the push or pull. Ask learners to identify each push or pull, identify its direction, and to describe its size.

Get things moving

Forces is a more straightforward topic when learners see and feel forces. Use the examples in the unit to get learners moving and observing the movement of objects.

Differentiation

In order to differentiate, you need to find out what learners know and can do at the beginning of a topic. Use the starter and early activities to get learners talking to find out what they know and can remember. Be prepared to then adjust your teaching to cater for what they already know and

can do. For example, begin the topic with a class poster, such as:

- things we already know, for example, for example, we need a force to push a chair
- things we would like to know about, for example, for example, very big forces.

Differentiation by outcome works well for science topics, like forces, that learners may not have studied for a year. Read the curriculum objectives that they should have studied already, and then begin with open-ended activities which will show you who has remembered previous learning, and who has not. For example, as you start a topic on forces, can learners suggest examples of different types of movement?

A stretch target will help challenge everyone in class. Share your learning objective and then the stretch target and encourage every learner to have a go at this target. For example, if your learning objective is to test how three different balls travel on different surfaces, add a stretch challenge such as design your own table to record the results.

2.1 Forces around us

Learning objectives	Learning intention	Success criteria
2Pf.01 Know that forces can change the movement of an object.	• We are going to learn that forces can make things move and make things stop.	• I can say how a push or pull can make things move or make things stop.
2TWSa.01 Describe what happened during an enquiry and if it matched their predictions.	• We are going to make predictions and say if they are correct.	• I can make predictions and say if they are correct.
2TWSc.04 Follow instructions safely when doing practical work.	• We are going to work in a safe way.	• I can work in a safe way.

LANGUAGE SUPPORT

In this topic learners should use simple connectives such as *because*, *if* and *when* to create sentences that describe how they use pushes and pulls to move things. Learners could write these sentences using the following pattern.

The (object) moves (when/if/because) I (push/pull) it.

For example, The ball moves when I push it. The chair moves if I pull it. The door handle moves because I push it.

Learners have learnt about different ways of moving in Stage 1, Unit 6, Topic 6.1. Encourage learners to use these as alternative verbs to *move* in their sentences.

For example, The ball rolls when I push it. The chair slides when I pull it. The door handle turns because I push it.

Ask learners to help make a display of things that they can move by pushing and pulling by bringing in pictures from home cut from newspapers or magazines and sticking them below the correct word.

Learners can use the Unit 2 Language worksheets to practice spelling some of the key words for this unit. On the worksheets there is a picture and a simple definition for each word.

away: moving away from something is getting less close to it

force: a push or a pull

launch: when something starts moving into the air or into water

pull/pulls: to try to move something towards you

push/pushes: to try to move something away from you

rocket: something that can fly to into space

stretch: change the shape of a material by pulling, when something gets longer

squashing: changing the shape of a material by pushing, when something gets shorter

towards: moving towards something is getting closer to it

Common misconceptions

Misconception	How to identify	How to overcome
Some learners may think that you cannot push or pull very heavy objects or objects that are fixed in place.	Ask learners to push or pull objects that are too heavy for them to move or objects that are fixed. Observe learners' reactions. Learners who say 'I can't push that,' have this misconception.	These learners are confusing push or pulling an object with making it move. Explain that you can push or pull very heavy objects and fixed objects but you cannot make them move because your push or pull is not large enough. Choose learners to demonstrate pushing on the classroom wall. Ask 'Is he/she pushing the wall?' then ask 'Is the wall moving?' Explain that a bigger force would be needed to move the wall.

Starter ideas

1 Getting started (10 minutes)

Resources: Learner's Book

Description: Show learners the push and pull signs pictured in the Learner's Book. Learners should work in pairs. Learners can take turns to show each other something that they can push in the classroom then something they can pull. Learners might demonstrate pushing and pulling a chair, a book or a pencil or pulling a door or a drawer open and pushing them closed.

Safety: Tell learners not to push or pull very heavy objects such as bookcases that might hurt them if they move.

Look out for learners who are not sure what to do, or who demonstrate pulling when asked to show pushing, etc. Check that these learners understand the differences between a push and a pull after the main activities of this topic.

2 Pushing or pulling (5 minutes)

Description: Ask learners to come to the front of the classroom and mime an action that uses pushing or pulling, for example, pulling a door open or pushing keys on a computer keyboard. The others can try to guess what the action is showing. Tell them to use the words 'pushing' or 'pulling' in their guesses.

Look out for learners who struggle to use the words 'pushing' or 'pulling' in their guesses or who use the wrong word. These learners will need support in the main activities to identify pushes and pulls and to learn to use this vocabulary.

Main teaching ideas

1 Activity: Using forces to move things and stop things (25 minutes)

Learning intention: We are going to learn that forces can make things move and make things stop.

We are going to work in a safe way.

Resources: Learner's Book, some large and small balls, a large space, some inflated balloons, some bowls of water and classroom chairs and pencils. Digital Classroom activity: Push or pull? (optional)

Description: Read the first few pages of Topic 2.1 in the Learner's Book with learners. This explains the difference between pushes and pulls and that forces can make things move and make things stop. Ask learners to talk about things that they like to do that involve forces and movement. You could ask these questions. 'Who likes to play in a play park? What do you like to play on? How do you make it move?'

Now read with learners Activity 1 Using forces to move things and stop things. This explains how to do the activity. Demonstrate, or ask learners to demonstrate, how pushes can be used to start or stop a ball moving. Take learners to a large space and allow them to investigate different ways of using pushes or pulls to make balls move and stop.

Safety: Tell learners to take care with the balls. Warn them to look at where other learners are in the space before making their ball move. Learners could work in pairs, but warn learners to only pass the ball to their partner when their partner is watching.

Choose pairs of learners to demonstrate making a ball move and stop.

Back in class, ask learners to investigate using pushes and pulls to make balloons, chairs, pencils and water move. You could encourage learners to blow air to push the balloons and the water by asking 'Can you push without using your hands?' Choose learners to demonstrate how they can move the different items.

> Digital Classroom: If you have access to Digital Classroom, use the activity 'Push or pull?' with learners. Learners can use this activity to label pictures of actions that involve pushing or pulling. The i button will explain how to use the activity.

> Differentiation ideas: Provide support for learners with developing English language skills by asking all learners to say 'push' or 'pull' out loud every time they pull or push and object.

Some learners could be challenged to investigate the effects of larger and smaller forces in this activity.

> Assessment ideas: After the activity, ask learners to talk about how pushes and pulls can make things move and stop in pairs or small groups. Listen to the discussions of some of the different groups to assess whether learners describe the pushes and pulls correctly.

2 Think like a scientist: Make a paper rocket launcher (20 minutes)

Learning intention: We are going to learn that forces can make things move and make things stop.

We are going to make predictions and say if they are correct.

We are going to work in a safe way.

Resources: Learner's Book, each pair of learners will need a small plastic bottle and a sheet of A4 paper

Description: Read 'Think like a scientist: Make a paper rocket launcher' with learners. This shows learners how they can make a paper rocket and use a plastic bottle to launch it. The bigger the push the higher the paper rocket goes.

Learners can make their own rocket, then use a small push or a big push to launch it. Make sure learners make predictions about how high the rocket will go before they launch it.

> Practical guidance: Demonstrate how to launch the rockets by hitting the bottle on both sides at the same time below the rocket. This will squash the bottle, quickly pushing air out. The air pushes the rocket upwards.

If any rocket is not launching correctly, twist the rocket hard over the top of the bottle to make sure there is a close fit. If the rocket is very loose on the bottle, air will escape through the gaps and not provide a big enough push on the rocket.

How high the rockets go is affected slightly by how far they are pushed onto the bottle before launching. Because of this, learners may find that some of their predictions are not correct. Explain to learners that it is important to say when their predictions are not correct because this can often lead to learning something new. In this activity, learners can make many predictions and many launches. Many of their predictions will be correct, so they should be happy to accept that some of their predictions are not.

Safety: Remind learners that they need to work safely. Tell them not to launch their rockets towards people.

During the activity, ask learners to peer assess by asking another learner to make a prediction, observing the launch and then asking that learner to say whether their prediction was correct. Learners should then say whether they agree with that learner or not.

> Differentiation ideas: Learners who need more support will benefit from teacher led demonstration of this activity after they have done the investigation. Ask these learners to make predictions then observe carefully while one learner launches the rocket with either a small or a

large push. Discuss with learners whether their predictions were correct.

Some learners could be challenged to measure how high the rockets go using metre rulers or a tape measure.

> **Assessment ideas:** Observe learners working to assess whether they can work in a safe way.

Talk with learners about their predictions, observe the launches and ask them to say whether their prediction was correct.

3 Workbook 2.1 (20 minutes)

Learning intention: We are going to learn that forces can make things move and make things stop.

Resources: Workbook

Description: Learners can use the Focus section to identify pushes and pulls. In the Practice activity, learners have to identify whether a force is large or small. In the Challenge activity, learners have to use key words from this topic to finish simple sentences.

> **Assessment ideas:** Assess individual learners by asking them to talk about how the objects in the Focus section move.

Plenary ideas

1 Reflection (5 minutes)

Resources: Learner's Book

Description: Read the Reflection in the Learner's Book with learners. Help learners to name the five senses, then ask them to think about which of the five human senses we use to observe forces.

Learners may say that we can see forces. Explain that actually we cannot see the forces, but we can see what the forces do. If something starts moving, or changes shape, it is because of a force, but we cannot see the force itself. Explain that we can sometimes hear the effects of a force too. The paper rockets investigation is a good example of this because learners will have heard the sound of the plastic bottles changing shape when they were squashed.

Ask learners to think about which other sense we might use to observe forces. Explain, if necessary, that we can feel forces with our sense of touch.

2 Moving house (10 minutes)

Resources: Video of whole houses being moved on trailers (search the internet for 'Moving entire house' or 'Extreme' house moving)

Description: Ask learners whether they think they could move the classroom by pushing it. Choose a learner to push the wall of the classroom to see if it will move. Ask 'Why is the wall not moving?' Explain, if necessary, that it would need a much larger push to make it move. Ask learners whether they think it would be possible to push or pull a whole house to make it move then show them a video of an entire house being moved on a trailer.

Safety: Check that the part of the wall you are asking learners to push is strong enough not to be affected by the force.

> **Assessment ideas:** Ask learners to say which of these things might be strong enough to push or pull a whole house a bulldozer, a lorry, an elephant, a person, a horse.

> ### CROSS-CURRICULAR LINKS

This topic links to physical education (P.E.) where pushes and pulls form the basis of controlled movement.

Homework ideas

Ask learners to draw and label things that they find at home that they can move by pushing or pulling.

Learners could use the Unit 2 Language worksheets to practise spelling words at home for a spelling test in class.

Ask learners to visit a play park with an adult and to talk about the pushes and pulls they use to make things move.

2.2 Changing shape

Learning objectives	Learning intention	Success criteria
2Pf.02 Know that forces can change the shape of an object.	• We are going to learn that forces can change the shape of some objects.	• I can say how forces can change the shape of some objects.
2TWSc.03 Take measurements in non-standard units.	• We are going to use objects to measure.	• I can use objects to measure.
2TWSa.02 Identify simple patterns in results, for example, increasing and decreasing patterns.	• We are going to look for patterns in our results.	• I can find patterns in my results.
2TWSc.06 Collect and record observations and/or measurements by annotating images and completing simple tables.	• We are going to record our results in a table.	• I can record my results in a table.

LANGUAGE SUPPORT

Learners will need to use simple, comparative and superlative adjectives in this topic for example, long, longer and longest/big, bigger, biggest.

Practise using these adjectives with learners by comparing sets of three different-sized objects in the classroom pointing to each one and asking learners to repeat the correct form of the adjective after you say it.

Display adjectives around the classroom in groups of three using the following layout.

big	long	small
bigger	longer	smaller
biggest	longest	smallest

height: how far from the bottom to the top of an object

investigate: to do a test or experiment to find something out

measure: to find the size or amount of something, for example length or time

object: something made of a material that you can see or touch

pattern: a change that is similar each time

results: what you observe or measure in an investigation

shape: the outline of an object for example, square, curved or flat

Common misconceptions

Misconception	How to identify	How to overcome
Some learners may think that a pattern can only be something visual like an arrangement of lines or shapes.	Show learners groups of numbers with a simple pattern such as times tables or a set of increasing numbers and ask 'Can you see a pattern in the numbers?'.	Explain that number patterns are different to visual patterns and that they can be very simple. For example, it might just be an increasing or decreasing pattern. Say 'The pattern might just be a getting bigger (or getting smaller) pattern – a set of numbers where each number is bigger (or smaller) than the last'.

Starter ideas

1 Getting started (10 minutes)

Resources: Class blackboard/whiteboard or large poster paper

Description: Explain to learners that this topic is about using forces to change the shape of things. Ask 'What do you do that changes the shape of things?'. Give learners the examples of changing the shape of food by chewing it or changing the shape of clothes by folding them, then ask learners to suggest other things. Record their ideas in a list on the board or large sheet of paper.

Learners might suggest the following: moving our bodies, opening a book, folding paper, cutting with a knife or saw, pushing or pulling clay, digging a hole in soil, etc.

Most correct suggestions involve movement actions. Be aware of learners who get confused by this and suggest different ways of moving that do not change the shape of something, for example, riding a bike, driving a car. Remind these learners that you are looking for actions that change the shape of something, not actions that make something move.

2 Which is the tallest? (10 minutes)

Resources: Two toy figures (people, animals etc.) that are similar in height and will stand upright on a table. Wooden or plastic counting bricks.

Description: Place two toy figures on two separate tables and ask 'Which of these is the tallest?'. Choose a learner to say which they think is tallest and ask the others whether they agree or disagree. Now ask learners to imagine that the toy figures cannot be moved. Show them the counting bricks and ask 'How can we use these to check which is the tallest?'. Discuss answers then choose learners to measure each figure with a tower of bricks. Talk about the height measurement of each figure then explain the difference between comparing and measuring.

Put the two figures side by side and say 'We can learn things in science by comparing'. Then put the figures next to the towers of bricks and say 'But it is better if we can learn by measuring. Measuring differences tells us more than just comparing them'.

Look out for learners who count the bricks incorrectly, or learners who count while moving a finger up the tower of bricks but do not point to or touch each brick in turn. Show these learners that, to count correctly, they must say the next number only when they touch the next brick.

Main teaching ideas

1 Think like a scientist 1: Finding patterns in results (30 minutes)

Learning intention: We are going to learn that forces can change the shape of some objects.

We are going to use objects to measure.

We are going to look for patterns in our results.

We are going to record our results in a table.

Resources: Learner's Book, counting bricks and some soft modelling clay or soft sticky tack or similar, prepared table of results for each group of learners as shown in the Learner's Book. Digital Classroom activity: Measuring height (optional)

Description: Learners can work in pairs or small groups for this activity. Read 'Think like a scientist 1: Finding patterns in results' with learners. This describes how to do the investigation, how to record the results and explains how to look for patterns in results.

Show learners how to roll the ball of clay between their hands to make it round and how to count bricks to measure the height from which they drop the ball. Tell learners to start by dropping the ball from a low height then increase the height each time. Two, four, six then eight bricks are suggested in the Learner's Book but, if learners are using small counting bricks, using five, ten, fifteen then twenty bricks will make a more observable difference in the results.

Tell learners to draw the shape of the ball of clay each time they drop it. They could also use simple, comparative and superlative adjectives to record the size of the change in shape of the clay ball each time; for example, small change in shape, large change in shape, larger change in shape, largest change in shape. Remind learners to make the clay back into a ball after each drop.

When all the results are recorded, ask learners to look for a pattern in their results. Say 'A pattern is when the result changes in a similar way each time. What happened to the ball each time you dropped it from a greater height?'. Ask learners to help complete this sentence that describes the pattern

'The higher we drop the ball from the... (*larger the change in shape of the ball*)'.

> **Digital Classroom:** If you have access to Digital Classroom, use the activity 'Measuring height' with learners. Learners can use this activity to practise using non-standard measures to measure height. The i button will explain how to use the activity.

> **Differentiation ideas:** Learners who need more support with making observations could use a larger ball of clay because the differences in the results will be more obvious.

Learners who need more support with measuring could use larger counting bricks.

This investigation could be simplified for learners who need lots of support with Thinking and Working Scientifically. Instead of measuring the height, three similar balls of clay could be dropped from a low, medium and high position and the results compared directly by looking at the three balls afterwards.

Some learners could be challenged to measure the height in centimetres using a ruler.

> **Assessment ideas:** Ask learners to use the pattern to predict what would happen if they dropped the ball from an even greater height. They could draw a pictures of their predictions on small whiteboards or paper. Learners should be able to predict that the change in shape would be even larger. This shows that they understand the pattern in the results. Learners who do not make this prediction should be given extra support in Think like a scientist 2 How do forces change rubber bands?

2 Worksheet 2.2A, 2.2B and 2.2C: Measuring practice (20 minutes)

Learning intention: We are going to use objects to measure.

Resources: Worksheet 2.2A, 2.2B and 2.2C, scissors, objects in the classroom to measure

Description: Learners use the counters on Worksheet 2.2A to measure objects around them. Alternatively, learners cut out the pictures from Worksheet 2.2B or 2.2C and use the line of squares or ruler to measure each picture.

> **Differentiation ideas:** Learners who need support with measuring could use Worksheet 2.2A. They should use the counters on the sheet to measure objects in the classroom.

Learners who are good at using non-standard measures could be challenged to use Worksheet 2.2C. Here they use a ruler to measure the same pictures as on Worksheet 2.2B.

> **Assessment ideas:** Work with learners who need support on Worksheet 2.2A. Assess these learners by checking their measurements.

Learners who use Worksheets 2.2B and 2.2C can be assessed when you mark their work.

3 Think like a scientist 2: How forces can change rubber bands (45 minutes)

Learning intention: We are going to learn that forces can change the shape of some objects.

We are going to use objects to measure.

We are going to look for patterns in our results.

We are going to record our results in a table.

Resources: Each group will need three or four books of a similar size, a large and a small rubber band, sticky notes, a paper clip and a prepared table of results as shown in Learner's Book.

Description: Read with learners 'Think like a scientist 2: How forces can change rubber bands'. This shows a picture of how to set up the investigation.

When learners have recorded their measurements ask 'What happens to the force on the rubber band when you add more books?'. Explain, if necessary, that the more books they use, the larger the pulling force on the rubber band. Then ask 'Did you see the pattern? What happened to the rubber band each time you made the pulling force larger?'. Ask learners to help complete this sentence that describes the pattern

'The larger the force the... (*longer the rubber band stretched*)'.

Now ask learners to look at their results and ask 'Can you see this pattern in your measurements?'. Show learners, if necessary, that every time they add a book, the length of the rubber band increases.

> **Practical guidance:** Show learners how use the large rubber band to make a bundle of books that can be attached to the small rubber band using a paper clip. Choose learners to demonstrate how to measure the length of the rubber band using the sticky notes attached to the leg of a table as shown in the pictures.

Put the learners into small groups and help each group set up their equipment. Tell learners to record their measurements each time they add a book. Make sure learners start by measuring the length of the small rubber band with no books attached then add one book and measure again each time. Recording the results in order as the weight is increased will make it easier to find the pattern.

Safety: Warn learners not to hold stretched rubber bands so they are pointing at anyone's eyes. This could be dangerous if the rubber band broke.

> **Differentiation ideas:** The investigation could be simplified for learners who need support by giving them one small, one medium and one large book. Ask them to measure the length of the rubber band when each book is hung from the rubber band by itself.

Some learners could be challenged to use the pattern in the results to predict what would happen if they added more books. Allow these learners to test their prediction if it is safe to do so. They may be surprised to find out that the rubber band gets to a point where it stops stretching. Tell these learners not to add any more books because the rubber band is near its breaking point.

> **Assessment ideas:** As learners are working, assess learners' measuring skills by asking each learner in a group to measure the rubber band or to check another learner's measurement.

4 Workbook 2.2 (20 minutes)

Learning intention: We are going to use objects to measure.

We are going to look for patterns in our results.

We are going to record our results in a table.

Resources: Workbook

Description: Learners can use the Focus exercise to practice the key words for this topic. The Practice activity allows them to practice measuring in non-standard units. The Challenge section checks they can spot patterns in results.

> **Assessment ideas:** You can assess learner's skills by marking their work.

Plenary ideas

1 Patterns in results (10 minutes)

Resources: Learner's Book

Description: Read the section in the Learner's Book that shows a girl called Lola whose table of results are not in a logical order. Instead of increasing the number of books by one each time Lola has gone from 0 to 3 to 1 to 2. Because of this Lola cannot see the pattern in the results.

Explain to learners that Lola has not been sensible when taking her measurements. Say 'Does the number of books go up by the same amount each time?'. Explain, if necessary, that the numbers in the 'number of books' column goes up and down by different amounts.

Rewrite the table of results on the board for learners, but put the results in a sensible order as shown here. Make it clear to learners that you are keeping each pair of numbers in the two columns together. As you write the table, write a '1' in the number of books column then ask 'How many sticky notes were there when there was one book?'. Show learners, if necessary, that the table in the Learner's Book shows that the number of sticky notes was 2. Repeat this for each row.

Number of books	Number of sticky notes
0	1
1	2
2	3
3	4

Now ask learners 'Is Lola right? Can you see a pattern in the results now?'.

Explain to learners, if necessary, that the pattern in the number of sticky notes is that it is going up by one each time.

Ask learners 'Why could Lola not see the pattern?'. Explain that it is important to take measurements in a sensible and logical order because it makes it easier to see if there is a pattern.

Remind learners to take their measurements in a sensible and logical way by making the same amount of change for each measurement.

⟩ Assessment ideas: At the start of this activity, challenge some learners to spot the pattern in the results in the Learner's Book.

After writing the simplified table of results on the board, ask learners to indicate whether they can see the pattern. Choose some learners to whisper to you what they think the pattern is before talking about it with the class.

⟩ Reflection ideas: Ask learners to think about these questions.

Did you add one book each time?

Was that a good way to do take the measurements?

2 What do you like to make? (10 minutes)

Resources: Learner's Book

Description: Show learners the pictures in the Learner's Book of bread, clay and wood being made into things. Ask 'What do you like to make?'. In the discussion that follows, ask learners to give examples of how they use forces when they are making things.

Learners might talk about helping with cooking, for example, *I use a spoon to stir*, or about making things with construction sets, for example, *I have to push the bricks together*, etc.

⟩ Assessment ideas: Give each learner a piece of paper and ask them to tell a classmate how they could use a force to change its shape. Say 'How can you change the shape of this paper?'. Ask learners to change the shape of their paper then choose learners to tell the class about the forces they used.

CROSS-CURRICULAR LINKS

This topic is a great opportunity for learners to develop their maths skills in number sequences. The results collected in the investigations can be used to teach learners to recognise, describe and extend number sequences. You could create some example tables with very simple sequences based on the investigations in this unit.

For example

Number of books	Length of rubber band
2	1
4	2
6	3
8	4

Learners can use these to practise describing and extending the number sequences. Here are some examples. The number of books goes up by two each time. The length of the rubber band goes up by one each time. For ten books, the rubber band will be 5 bricks long.

Homework ideas

Ask learners to look for things at home they use forces to change the shape of. Learners could make or continue a list like the one used in the starter activity What do you know already? Alternatively, learners could draw pictures of the things they find and label them.

Challenge learners to find some small objects they can use at home to use as non-standard measures. They could use bottle tops, buttons, paper clips, felt tip pens, etc. Ask them to measure the length or height of some larger objects using their non-standard measure. You could give them a table of results to fill in.

Topic Worksheets

Worksheets 2.2A, 2.2B and 2.2C

Learners who need more support use the counters on Worksheet 2.2A to measure objects around them.

Alternatively, learners cut out the pictures from Worksheet 2.2B and use the squares to measure the height of each picture.

More confident learners can be challenged to use Worksheet 2.2C and use the l ruler to measure the height of each picture.

2.3 Changing speed

LEARNING PLAN

Learning objectives	Learning intention	Success criteria
2Pf.03 Recognise that things will only speed up, slow down or change direction when something else causes them to do so.	• We are going to find out how forces make things go faster or slower.	• I can say how forces can make something move faster or slower.
2TWSp.01 Ask questions about the world around us and talk about how to find answers.	• We are going to ask questions about how to make things go faster or slower.	• I can ask a questions about how to make something move faster or slower.
2TWSa.02 Identify simple patterns in results, for example, increasing and decreasing patterns.	• We are going to look for patterns in our results.	• I can find patterns in results.
2TWSc.02 Use given equipment appropriately.	• We are going to investigate carefully and safely.	• I can investigate carefully and safely.
2TWSc.04 Follow instructions safely when doing practical work.		

LANGUAGE SUPPORT

Continuing from Topic 2.2, learners will again use simple, comparative and superlative adjectives in this topic, for example, fast, faster, fastest and slow, slower, slowest. These could be displayed as described in Topic 2.2.

Learners will use comparative adjectives to describe patterns observed in results in this topic

for example, *The bigger the push, the faster the ball moves.* Support them by using and displaying these sentence structures.

The _____ the push, the _____ the _____ moves.

The _____ the pull, the _____ the _____ moves.

Learners will ask questions in this topic. Talk with them about identifying questions by looking for question marks and the different words that can be used to start a question; *who, when, why, what, where* and *how*. Ask learners to find questions in simple texts and help them to write their own questions using the sentence structure *How do you make _____ go faster/slower?*

brakes: the parts of a bike or other vehicle that make it slow down

explain: to make something clear

fast, faster: to take little time to move to a new place

pedals: the parts of a bike you push with your feet to make it move

slow, slower: to take a long time to move to a new place

slow down, get slower: when something starts to move less quickly

speed: how fast something is moving

speed up, get faster: when something starts to move more quickly

Common misconceptions

Misconception	How to identify	How to overcome
Most learners will have the misconception that forces are not needed to make most moving objects slow down. They will think that slowing down is something that moving objects do when the pushing force making them move is removed. For example, they will think that no forces are involved when a bicycle slows down and eventually stops because you stop pedalling.	In the activities in this topic, look out for learners who say that you do not need to make an object slow down, it will just slow down by itself.	One of forces that makes objects appear to slow down 'by themselves' is friction. Friction is introduced in the curriculum at Stage 3. Explain to learners that there is a force that we cannot see between an object and the surface it is moving over. Tell them that it is called 'friction'. You could ask learners to rub their hands together, and explain that this is the same force that makes your hands feel warm when you rub them together. The other force that slows moving objects is air resistance, which is introduced at Stage 5. Explain that a moving object has to move through the air. Pushing air out of the way makes a small force that we can't see that pushes against the moving object.

Starter ideas

1 Getting started (10 minutes)

Resources: Learner's Book

Description: Ask learners to talk in pairs, or threes, about how the girl could make the bike go faster or slower. Choose learners to tell the class their group's ideas and ask the others to show whether they agree or disagree. Choose individuals to give reasons why they agree or disagree. Explain, if necessary, that to go faster, the girl must push harder on the pedals and to slow down she can pull on the brakes.

Look out for learners who say that if she stops pedalling the bike will slow down by itself. Explain that they are right that the bike will slow down but not 'by itself'. The girl and the bike have to push air out of the way to move and the air pushes back on them and makes them slow down.

2 How a bike works (10–15 minutes)

Resources: Learner's Book, a child's bike with pedals and brakes (optional)

Description: Read with learners the section of the Learner's Book that describes how to make a bike speed up and slow down. Ask learners to talk about their own experiences of riding bikes. If possible, show a real bicycle and identify the pedals and brakes. Choose a learner to pretend that they have never ridden a bicycle and ask the others to explain to this learner how they would ride a bike and how they could make it go faster or go slower.

Safety: Do not ask any learners to ride the bicycle.

Explain that pushing harder on the pedals will make the bike speed up and pulling on the brake levers will make the bike slow down.

Note: It is not necessary to explain how the brakes work, but some learners may be interested to see how pulling the brake lever pulls a cable which in turn pulls brake block onto the rim of the wheel (or onto a special disc if the bike has disc brakes). You could explain that the blocks pushing on the wheel (or disc) make a force that slows the wheel down. This is called friction. Some bicycles have a special system where you have to pedal backwards to apply the brake. This is called a coaster brake and the mechanism is hidden inside the wheel.

Some learners might talk about dragging their feet on the ground to slow down. Explain that this does make a slowing down force as they have to push on the ground and the grip (friction) between their foot and the ground slows the bike down. Explain that this is not a safe way to make a bike slow down because they could get hurt and it will also wear out their shoes.

3 Digital Classroom song: That's a force (15 minutes)

Resources: Digital Classroom

> **Digital Classroom:** If you have access to the Digital Classroom component, you can use the song 'That's a force' with learners. Learners can watch and join in with the chorus of this song about forces. The i button will explain how to use the song.

Main teaching ideas

1 Think like a scientist 1: Asking questions about speed (15 minutes)

Learning intention: We are going to ask questions about how to make things go faster or slower.

Resources: Learner's Book, sticky notes, poster paper

Description: Read with learners 'Think like a scientist 1', which illustrates the sentence structure below and shows how it can be used to ask questions about speed.

How do you make... (a ball) ...go faster/slower?

Ask learners to look at the picture of children playing in a park in the Learner's Book and use the activities they see to ask new questions about speed. For example, 'How do you make a paper aeroplane go slower?'.

Ask learners to record their questions on sticky notes and display them together on a class questions poster.

Find out more about what learners already know by asking them to answer some of the questions if they can. Then ask learners if they can use the sentence structure to ask similar questions about activities that they like to do themselves. These questions can also be recorded on sticky notes and added to the class poster.

2 FORCES AND MOVEMENT

Differentiation ideas: Some learners could be supported by giving them a set of prepared sticky notes or cards as shown in the Learner's Book. They can then make different questions by changing the cards used in the sentence.

Learners with good English language skills could be challenged to check the questions written by other learners for capital letters and question marks. These learners should point out any mistakes to other learners who can then make their own corrections.

> **Assessment ideas:** You can assess some learners by listening to the questions they ask. Ask all learners to write their names with their questions on their sticky notes. You can then assess learner's questions after the activity.

2 Think like a scientist 2: Blow the ball (30 minutes)

Learning intention: We are going to find out how forces make things go faster or slower.

We are going to look for patterns in our results.

We are going to investigate carefully and safely.

Resources: Learner's Book, a lightweight ball for each pair of learners, (sponge balls, ball pool balls or table tennis balls are ideal), a table or other flat surface

> **Practical Guidance:** Read with learners 'Think like a scientist 2' in the Learner's Book which shows how to use blowing to create a small force that will slow down a moving ball. Ask learners to work in pairs. They should sit at opposite ends of a table as shown. One learner should roll the ball gently across the table, the other should blow the ball as it gets close to make it slow down. Say to learners 'When you blow the ball the air pushes against the ball. This small force makes the ball slow down'.

Safety: Talk with learners about using equipment in an appropriate and safe way. Tell them not to throw the balls.

Next ask 'Can you make the ball get faster by blowing it?'. There are two ways to do this. Learners can start with a stationary ball and blow it to make it move. The ball's speed increases from zero so the ball is speeding up. Alternatively, a learner could roll the ball slowly away from themselves and then blow from behind it as it rolls to make it roll faster.

Learners can peer assess by watching another pair to check they can make the ball slow down and speed up.

The Learner's Book shows a girl who is trying to describe the pattern that can observed in how the ball moves. Ask 'What happens if you give the ball a small push away from you?' then 'What happens if you give it a bigger push?' and lastly 'What happens if you give it a very big push?'. Discuss learners' answers and explain, if necessary, that with a small push the ball moves slowly, with a bigger push it moves faster and with a very big push it moves very fast. Now ask learners to try to finish the girl's sentence 'The bigger the push, the ...' If necessary, help learners reach the conclusion that the bigger the push the faster the ball moves.

> **Differentiation ideas:** Learners who find it difficult to control their blowing could be given a drinking straw to blow through.

Learners with a good understanding of forces could be challenged by asking them to predict the effect of blowing balls of different weights and sizes.

> **Assessment ideas:** After the activity ask learners to work individually to copy and complete the following sentence on a small whiteboard or on rough paper.

The smaller the push the...

Learners who can complete the sentence correctly (*The smaller the push the slower the ball moves*) can find patterns in results.

3 Workbook 2.3 (20 minutes)

Learning intention: We are going to find out how forces make things go faster or slower.

Resources: Workbook

Description: Learners can use the Focus activity to identify which forces will make things move faster or slower. The Practice section asks learners to complete sentences to describe how to speed up and slow down a bicycle. In the Challenge activity, they have to identify how Sofia can speed up or slow down a roundabout.

> **Assessment ideas:** You can assess whether learners can identify forces that make things move faster or slower when you mark their work.

Plenary ideas

1   Flap a fish (15 minutes)

Resources: Large fish shapes cut from newspaper, large books to use as fans

Description: Show learners how to wave a large book up and down to push air towards a paper fish on the ground. The more force used to push the air the faster the fish will move.

Choose two learners to have a 'Flap the fish' race. Each learner has a fish and a book. The fish that crosses the line first is the winner.

Ask learners to say why the winning fish moved faster. Explain, if necessary, that the learner pushing the winning fish was using a bigger force

Safety: Make sure that learners who are watching keep well back from the learners waving the books.

> **Assessment ideas:** Ask learners to suggest ways of moving the fish even faster. Learners might suggest using an electric fan or pushing the fish with a stick. Ask them to explain why this could make the fish move faster to assess whether they can explain that a larger force will make them move faster.

2   Do forces always make things move? (10 minutes)

Description: Choose a learner to come to the front. Stand facing each other and hold your hands out so your hands are touching the learner's hands palm to palm. Demonstrate what happens if the learner pushes with their hands and you push back with the same force. Ask 'Who is pushing?'. Agree with learners that both people are pushing, then ask 'If we are both pushing, why are we not moving?' Explain, if necessary, that because you are both pushing with the same size force, but in opposite directions, the forces are balanced. Explain that when forces are balanced, things do not speed up or slow down.

Safety: Instruct the learner helping with the demonstration not to use a very big force to make it easy to balance the forces without any risk of injury.

> **Assessment ideas:** Ask learners to say which direction you would move if your pushing force was larger than the learner's force or if their pushing force was larger than yours.

CROSS-CURRICULAR LINKS

You could make a link with road safety in the topic. Talk with learners about crossing the road safely and explain the pattern that faster cars take longer to stop than cars travelling more slowly. Help learners to recognise that, because of this, roads with faster traffic are more dangerous to cross.

Homework ideas

Ask learners to draw a picture of themselves or other children doing an activity that uses forces to make something speed up or slow down. They could draw riding a bike, roller skating, playing football or basketball, doing gymnastic, swimming, playing with toy cars, etc. Challenge some learners to write a sentence about making things move faster and a sentence about making things move slower.

Show learners how to play a game outside where they use some of the key words in this unit to give instructions to others. Choose one learner to give the instructions speed up, slow down, get faster, get slower, stop while other learners move around the playground following the instructions. Learners could play this game again at home with a friend or with an adult.

2.4 Changing direction

Learning objectives	Learning intention	Success criteria
2Pf.03 Recognise that things will only speed up, slow down or change direction when something else causes them to do so.	• We are going to find out how forces make things change direction.	• I can say how forces can make something change direction.
2TWSp.02 Make predictions about what they think will happen.	• We are going to predict what we think will happen.	• I can predict what I think will happen.
2TWSa.01 Describe what happened during an enquiry and if it matched their predictions.	• We are going to say if our predictions are correct or not.	• I can say if my predictions are correct or not.
2TWSm.03 Describe the difference between a diagram and a picture.	• We are going to find out how a diagram is different to a picture.	• I can say how a diagram is different to a picture.

LANGUAGE SUPPORT

Learners can draw their predictions in this topic, but they will need to use the future tense to talk about them. Help them to do this using the simple grammatical form that uses the word *will* before the verb in a sentence to refer to future intention. For example,

The ball *will* go that way.

The force *will* make the ball turn.

diagram: a drawing that shows important information and explains this with labels and arrows, lines and text

direction: a path towards or away from something

turn: when something moving changes to move on a different path

Common misconceptions

Misconception	How to identify	How to overcome
Some learners may think that for every object to move in a certain direction, a force in that direction is needed. This is true when we make other objects move – you push a ball in the direction you want it to go – but the opposite is true for making ourselves move.	In the 'Activity: Feel the force', ask learners to say which way they have to push to change direction. Look out for learners who say that they have to push in the new direction.	Explain that when we move ourselves we have to push in the opposite direction. Ask a learner to stand close to a wall facing away from it then push on the wall behind them with their hands. This will demonstrate that a backwards push makes us move forwards. Then ask learners to run in a straight line then quickly turn left. Ask them to think about what they do with their feet. Their feet with push to the right to make them turn left.

Starter ideas

1 Getting started (10 minutes)

Resources: Learner's Book

Description: Show learners the picture in the Learner's Book that show a boy on roller skates being pulled by another boy towards a gate. Ask learners 'What is going to happen?'. If learners say that the boy can just stop, say 'What if he is going too fast to stop? How can he not crash into the gate?'. Show learners that the road goes round the corner and ask 'How could the boy go round the corner?'. Explain, if necessary, that his friend must pull him around the corner. Say 'His friend can use a force to make him turn'. Then ask 'Can his friend push him to make him turn? Can his friend pull him to make him turn?'. If required, explain that the friend could push or pull, but the force would have to be along the road that goes around the corner.

Look out for learners who think that the boy could just stop. Ask whether they can always stop straight away when moving fast. Explain that the faster you are moving, the longer it takes to slow down. You could take learners into the playground to demonstrate this by asking a learner to run until you say 'stop'. The other learners should watch where the runner is when you say stop and where they are when they do stop.

2 What can forces do? (10 minutes)

Resources: Small whiteboard or paper, class whiteboard/blackboard or large poster paper, Learner's Book

Description: Remind learners that this unit has been all about forces. Ask them to use small whiteboards or paper to draw or write a list of the different things that forces can do. Learners may find this easier of they start by sharing some ideas in a small group before drawing or writing.

Next ask learners to show you some of the things they have drawn or tell you some of the things they have written. Record these under three different headings on the class board or on a large poster in a table as shown below.

Forces can...		
make things move and stop	make things change shape	make things go faster or slower
For example, open a door, move a chair	For example, squash a cushion, twist paper	For example, pedal a bike, kick a ball

When you have two or three examples from the learners under each heading say to learners 'Today we are going to learn about one more thing that forces can do. Forces can also make things change direction'. Read with learners the section in the Learner's Book that show a boat changing direction. Use this to explain the meaning of the word 'direction'. Choose two learners to demonstrate by walking across the classroom and then changing direction when you say 'Change direction'.

Look out for learners who draw or write about changes that do not involve forces, for example, making things hot or cold. Explain that these are changes but they do not need a push or a pull to make them happen.

Main teaching ideas

1 Activity: Feel the force (20 minutes)

Learning intention: We are going to find out how forces make things change direction.

Resources: Learner's Book, a playground or other large space, video recording device (optional)

Description: Read with learners the section in the Learner's Book that explains that forces are needed to make things change direction. Then read 'Activity: Feel the force', which explains how to play a changing direction game. Learners can run around in the playground but they have to change direction every time you say 'Change'. Ask learners to think about what their feet do when they change direction quickly. Choose a learner to demonstrate that, when running then turning left, you have to push to the right with your right foot. This creates the push that allows you to change direction. If possible, video a learner changing direction then show this to learners when back in class. Pause the video to show the push or show the video in slow motion if possible.

Safety: Tell learners to keep a safe distance from each other and make sure they look where they are going to avoid accidents. If the space is small, learners can take turns to try this out in groups.

> **Differentiation ideas:** Challenge some learners to link this activity to the previous topic by asking them to compare the force needed to change direction slightly while running and the force needed to change direction completely. Help learners to see the pattern: the bigger the push the bigger the change in direction.

> **Assessment ideas:** Each time you stop the game, choose learners to tell you how they changed direction. Ask them to use the words push, pull or force in their answers.

2 Think like a scientist: This way or that way? (30 minutes)

Learning intention: We are going to find out how forces make things change direction.

We are going to predict what we think will happen.

We are going to say if our predictions are correct or not.

We are going to find out how a diagram is different to a picture.

Resources: Learner's Book, each group will need a large sheet of poster paper or newspaper, two marker pens of different colours and a ball, video recording devices (optional) Digital Classroom Science investigators video: How can we change the movement of a ball? (optional)

Description: Read with learners 'Think like a scientist: This way or that way?', which explains how to do the investigation and record predictions on a diagram. This also explains how a diagram is different to a picture.

Learners should work in pairs or small groups. They should draw a ball and an arrow, showing the direction they will roll the ball, on their piece of paper. They should then add an arrow to show the direction they will push the ball while it is moving. Next, in a different colour, they can draw an arrow to show where they predict the ball will go.

One learner should now roll the ball over the diagram and the other should add a gentle push as shown by their push arrow. Learners should do this several times and observe which direction the ball goes in. Ask learners to record the result on their diagram using another arrow drawn in the first colour used. Using the colours this way means that the only arrow in a different colour is the prediction. This will make it easier for learners to see whether their prediction matched what happens.

Safety: Make sure learners handle the balls safely indoors and only roll them gently to keep other learners safe.

Ask groups of learners to pair up and peer assess by looking at the diagrams of other learners. Ask learners to talk about whether the predictions were correct or not.

If you have access to video recording devices, learners could use these to video some of the investigations which you could watch and discuss together at the end of the investigation.

Note: It is not necessary for the ball to travel exactly along the learners' prediction arrow for them to consider their prediction correct. Make it clear to learners that if the ball moves in a direction that is close to their prediction they can say that their prediction was about right.

Learners' diagrams could be displayed in the classroom or stapled together to make a giant book which could go on display.

> **Digital Classroom:** If you have access to the Digital Classroom component, watch the Science investigators video 'How can we change the movement of a ball?' with learners. Pause the video so learners can answer questions at the 'Pause for thought' sections. The i button will explain how to use the video.

> **Differentiation ideas:** Learners who need more support with making prediction could work together as a larger group guided by an adult.

Challenge some learners to investigate the effect of a small, medium and large pushing force in the direction they have drawn. Each results should be slightly different.

> **Assessment ideas:** Observe learners during the peer assessment activity to check they can say whether their prediction is correct or not. Ask learners to write their names on their diagrams which can then be assessed when marked.

3 Workbook 2.4 (15 minutes)

Learning intention: We are going to find out how forces make things change direction.

We are going to predict what we think will happen.

We are going to say if our predictions are correct or not.

Resources: Workbook (for the Challenge exercise, a piece of paper for each learner)

Description: The Focus activity is an opportunity for learners to practise recognising and spelling some of the key words for this unit. In the Practice exercise, they are asked to draw an arrow to show the direction of the force needed to change the direction of a moving ball so that it goes into a net. In the Challenge activity, learners will investigate letting a piece of paper fall in different ways, making predictions then checking them before completing sentences about the paper changing direction.

› **Assessment ideas:** You can assess learners by marking their work.

4 Balloon in the wind (10–20 minutes)

Learning intention: We are going to find out how forces make things change direction.

Resources: A balloon filled with air not helium on a string about 1 m long, a large outdoor space and a windy day, Worksheets 2.4A, 2.4B and 2.4C (optional)

Description: Take learners outside on a windy day to observe how a balloon moves in the wind. Start by letting the balloon hang down on its string and watch as the wind moves the balloon around. Ask learners to say what force is making the balloon move. If necessary, explain that it is the moving air pushing on the balloon.

Next, ask learners to stand in a large circle and let the balloon go in the middle of the circle. Watch where the balloon goes and ask a learner to catch it when it gets to the edge of the circle. Talk with learners about where the balloon went. Ask 'Why did the balloon change direction?'. Explain that gusts of wind usually come from slightly different directions, so each time there is a gust of wind, the balloon gets pushed in a different direction.

Safety: Tell learners not to run after the balloon. Make sure they stand still to observe.

The majority of learners could now complete Worksheet 2.4B, which asks them to draw the path of a balloon as it is pushed in different ways by four children and put sentences that describe the forces in the correct order. Worksheets 2.4A or 2.4C could be used for learners who need more support or more challenging material respectively.

› **Differentiation ideas:** Learners who need more support with English could complete Worksheet 2.4A, which asks them to draw the path of a balloon as it is pushed in different ways by four children and choose the correct word to finish a simple sentence.

Learners who have a good understanding of forces could be asked to complete Worksheet 2.4C, which shows the path of the balloon and asks learners to draw an arrow for each person to show which direction they pushed the balloon in.

› **Assessment ideas:** You can assess learners understanding of forces making things change directions by questioning learners during the outdoor activity and by marking their worksheets.

Plenary ideas

1 Diagrams or pictures? (10 minutes)

Resources: Learners' diagrams from Think like a scientist 1 This way or that way?

Description: Show learners some of the diagrams they drew in Think like a scientist 1 This way or that way?, which show the path of the moving ball and their predictions. Ask 'Are these pictures or diagrams?'. To help learners work out the difference ask 'Do they show what the ball looked like? Do they show who rolled the ball and who pushed the ball?' then explain that a picture of the investigation might show these things, but a diagram does not.

Ask learners 'For the investigation, it does not matter who rolls the ball. Why not? It does not matter what the ball looked like. Why not?'. Explain, if necessary, that these things will not change the investigation. They have no effect on the results. Explain that a diagram only shows the details that are important for the investigation.

› **Assessment ideas:** Note any learners who still identify the diagram as a picture at the end of the activity.

> Reflection ideas: Ask learners to discuss why they think diagrams are more useful than pictures for learning science.

2   Wheelchair basketball (10 minutes)

Resources: Learner's Book, smooth floor or large piece of cardboard or a thin gymnastics floor mat

Description: Read with learners the section in the Learner's Book that shows people playing wheelchair basketball. Ask 'How do you think they can make their wheelchairs change direction?'. Help learners to work out the answer by asking one learner to sit cross-legged on a smooth surface.

Ask the learner to stay cross-legged and try to spin themselves around to face a different direction. Ask the others to observe what forces the learner uses. Repeat this if necessary to demonstrate that the learner can turn by pushing on the floor with one hand and pulling on the floor with the other.

Explain that this is how a wheelchair can turn, by using a push and a pull on the opposite wheels or even by using a large push on one wheel and a small push on the other.

If your classroom does not have a smooth floor, then a large piece of cardboard or a thin gymnastics mat would work instead.

Safety: Make sure the surface the learner sits on is clean and free from sharp objects.

> Assessment ideas: At the end of this activity ask learners 'What do things need to change direction?'.

CROSS-CURRICULAR LINKS

This topic has clear links with movement in physical education (PE). Learners could help to work out a dance that involves changes of direction. Encourage them to come up with contrasting movements in opposite directions; up/down, left/right and forward/back.

Homework ideas

Ask learners to draw and label pictures of things they do at home that involve changing direction.

Ask learners to find a picture of an object, animal or person changing direction. This could be from a newspaper, in a book or from the internet. Ask learners to cut out or print out the pictures and add arrows to show the forces needed to change direction. If the picture is in a book, or if they cannot print it out, the learner should be prepared to show the picture and describe the forces involved to the rest of the class.

Topic worksheets

Worksheets 2.4A, 2.4B and 2.4C

Learners who need more support with English could complete Worksheet 2.4A, which asks them to draw the path of a balloon as it is pushed in different ways by four children and choose the correct word to finish a simple sentence.

The majority of learners should be able to complete Worksheet 2.4B, which asks them to draw the path of a balloon as it is pushed in different ways by four children and put sentences that describe the forces in the correct order.

Learners who have a good understanding of forces could be asked to complete Worksheet 2.4C, which shows the path of the balloon and asks learners to draw an arrow for each.

PROJECT: HOW PEOPLE USE FORCES

2SIC.03 Know that everyone uses science and identify people who use science professionally.

Read with learners the Unit 2 Project in the Learner's Book, which shows a school caretaker and describes how he uses forces in his job. Talk with them about other people who work in school and how they use forces such as teachers, cleaners, cooks and other kitchen staff.

Then talk about the things that the learners do themselves at school that uses forces, such as pushing and pulling a pencil to write, turning the pages of a book and moving in the playground.

Ask learners to choose some people who work in school and make a list of the things they do that use forces. Learners could draw pictures of the different tasks that people do and label them with the pushes and pulls involved.

If possible, learners could take photographs of people doing jobs around school that use forces and then label the pushes and pulls involved on the photographs.

Note: You should check with other staff in school that they consent to having their photograph taken and used in this way before allowing learners to take any photographs.

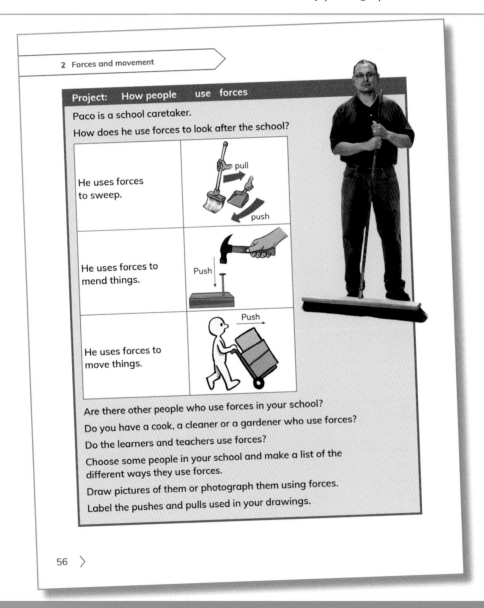

>3 Getting materials right

Unit plan

Topic	Approximate number of learning hours	Outline of learning content	Resources
3.1 Natural and made materials	2	Finding out where materials come from, which are natural and which are made. Using secondary information sources.	**Learner's Book:** Activity: Natural or made materials? Think like a scientist: Finding out where materials come from **Workbook:** Topic 3.1 **Digital Classroom:** Activity – Natural or made?
3.2 Properties of materials	1.5	Investigating the properties of materials. Sorting materials by their properties.	**Learner's Book:** Think like a scientist 1: Questions about materials Think like a scientist 2: Using a Venn diagram for sorting **Workbook:** Topic 3.2 **Digital Classroom:** Song – Sort it out Activity – Material characteristics
3.3 Using the right material	1	Finding out how a material's properties determine what that material can be used for.	**Learner's Book:** Activity 1: Sensible and silly materials Activity 2: Why is that material useful? **Workbook:** Topic 3.3 **Teacher's Resource:** ⬇ Worksheets: 3.3A, 3.3B, 3.3C **Digital Classroom:** Activity – Why do we use...?

Topic	Approximate number of learning hours	Outline of learning content	Resources
3.4 Testing materials	2	Investigating waterproof fabrics and the strength of paper. Drawing block graphs.	**Learner's Book:** Think like a scientist 1: Which fabric is best for an umbrella? Think like a scientist 2: Which paper makes the strongest bag? **Workbook:** Topic 3.4 **Teacher's Resource:** ⬇ Worksheets: 3.4A, 3.4B, 3.4C
3.5 Changing materials	2	Observing changes to materials. Planning an investigation.	**Learner's Book:** Think like a scientist 1: Observing toast. Think like a scientist 2: Can you stop peeled fruit going brown? **Workbook:** Topic 3.5 **Digital Classroom:** Video – The effect of heating different materials

Across Unit resources

Learner's Book:

Project: Materials can damage the Earth

Check your progress quiz

Teacher's Resource:

⬇ Language worksheets 1 and 2

⬇ Diagnostic check

Digital Classroom:

⬇ End-of-unit quiz

BACKGROUND KNOWLEDGE

Learners should have already learnt about materials in Stage 1 Unit 3. In Stage 1, they learnt about the names of different materials, some material properties and how materials can be tested and sorted into groups for recycling.

There are many different materials. Materials can have many different properties. Often, but not always, the properties are dependent on the shape of the material. For example, steel can be made into a flexible spring or a rigid bar, but steel is always hard. Encourage learners to make generalisations. For example, some metal is flexible, most plastic is waterproof. When sorting materials, learners will make judgements on whether an object or material has a particular property by comparing it with other materials. Therefore, the judgements they make are relative. For example, a wooden stick may be 'strong' when compared to paper tissue, but it may be considered weak when compared to the leg of a table. It may be helpful to ask learners to arrange materials or objects in order, such as weakest to strongest, etc.

We often use material by simply changing the shape. For example, wood is cut and sanded and pieces glued together to make a chair, and cotton is spun to line up the threads which are then woven together to make cotton fabric.

We can also change materials by heating or cooling them. For some materials, this can cause a reaction as the material combines with others to make new materials. This happens when bread is heated. Materials in the bread react together to make new materials with different flavours.

For other materials, changing their temperature simply causes them to change to a different state of matter. For example, water can freeze to make ice or evaporate to make steam. A change of state is not a change that makes a new material. Ice and steam are still water, but in its solid and gaseous state. Changes of state are reversible as no new materials are produced.

Natural materials can be used to make other materials. For example, paper is made from wood, plastic from oil and glass is made from sand.

TEACHING SKILLS FOCUS

Language awareness

Develop vocabulary

There is a lot of language linked to this topic, for example, the many names of materials learners will experience. You will usually be using group names for different categories of materials, for example, metal, wood, plastic, rock, etc. However, at times you may want to teach specific names, for example, limestone, chalk, granite. You don't need to know the name of every material, but it is worth learning more yourself and being selective with the ones you teach to the class. Generally, children love learning new terms.

Focus attention

Listen to learners taking about materials and to their questions, which you can then use to stimulate thinking. For example, 'That's interesting, might there be other liquids that do that?'. Keep the lesson objective and key vocabulary in mind so that you can, from time to time, refocus learners. For example, 'We called that a mixture, remind me of the other mixtures have we talked about.'

Active learning

The topic of materials presents many options for active learning, for example, whether materials are suitable or not for a function. An example is 'Which material is suitable for making a window?'. Challenge learners to think of unsuitable materials as well, for example, what materials would be unsuitable for a worker's helmet? They could consider glass, jelly, metal, chocolate or plastic. Can they say why materials are unsuitable? Can they be specific about the characteristics of a good material for a particular task? For example, material for a helmet should be light, strong, can be shaped, can be made in bright colours.

CONTINUED

Reflect on your teaching

You need to have good subject and professional knowledge of science and science teaching. How strong is your personal subject knowledge? Does it vary across different aspects of science? In your stronger areas, how does your confidence affect your teaching? In order to become more confident, make sure you check your personal subject knowledge. Take note of advice about possible misconceptions learners may have, and the different approaches to teaching suggested in different topics.

3.1 Natural and made materials

LEARNING PLAN

Learning objectives	Learning intention	Success criteria
2Cm.01 Understand that some materials occur naturally and others are manufactured.	• We are going to learn about where materials come from. • We are going to learn which materials are natural and which materials have been made by people.	• I can say where some materials come from. • I can name two or more natural materials and two or more materials that have been made.
2TWSc.05 Use a given secondary information source to find an answer to a question. **2TWSp.01** Ask questions about the world around us and talk about how to find answers.	• We are going to use books, videos or the internet to answer questions.	• I can use a book, video or the internet to answer questions.

LANGUAGE SUPPORT

This topic includes an activity where learners search for information from books, videos or the internet. This activity provides an opportunity for learners to read and explore short, simple non-fiction texts. Show learners how to find relevant information by scanning the text for important words. You could also show them how to find information in books using the contents page or index.

Show learners how to decode new words found in texts or videos using context and picture clues.

This unit includes many material names which are nouns and properties which are adjectives. Learners can use the Unit 3 Language worksheets to practise spelling these new words.

cotton: a fluffy white material that comes from a plant and is made into a fabric

glass: a clear material we use to make windows

natural: can be found in nature, not made by people

oil: a black liquid material that is found underground that can burn

paper: a material we can use to write on

plastic: a material that comes in many different colours and shapes

rubber: a material that can bend easily and comes from the rubber tree

sand: loose yellow or brown material made up of very small pieces of rock

water: a clear liquid material that we need to drink, the sea and rivers are water

wood: a material that comes from the trunk of a tree

Common misconceptions

Misconception	How to identify	How to overcome
In everyday English the word 'material' can be used to mean 'fabric'. This may confuse learners.	Early in this topic tell learners to point to materials in the classroom. Look out for learners who point to fabrics.	Explain to learners that in science 'fabric' is the word used for cloth and that the word 'material' means 'what something is made of'. Take care not to confuse learners by using the word material incorrectly yourself.
Some learners may confuse an object with the material it is made from.	Point to objects made of a single material or pictures of them and ask learners 'What is the name of this material?'.	Explain to learners that they have given the name of the object. Remind them what the word material means. Ask them to repeat the word and listen for it in the question. Help these learners to identify the material the object is made of by talking about what is looks like or feels like. Talking about what it is not made of can help. Ask 'Is the table made of paper?'.
Some learners may think that if a material has been in a factory then it is not natural.	In Think like a scientist 1 Finding out where materials come from, ask learners whether they agree that cotton is a natural material.	Explain to learners that there are different types of factories. Some change one material into a different material like the paper, glass and plastic factories as pictured in the Learner's Book. Others take a material and simply change its shape. The cotton factory pictured is an example; the material is still the same at the end but its shape is different. If necessary, compare this to a chair made of wood. The wooden material is still natural, even though its shape has been changed by a person.

Starter ideas

1 Getting started (10 minutes)

Resources: Learner's Book

Description: Ask learners 'Do you know what paper is made from?'. Discuss their responses. Ask learners whether they agree or disagree with any answers given by others. Explain, if necessary, that paper is made from wood. Wood is taken to a factory where it is broken up into very small fibres and soaked in water. Then the mixture is rolled out very thin and dried to make paper.

Ask learners 'Do you know where wood comes from?'. Explain, if necessary, that wood come from the stems of trees called 'trunks'.

Ask learners to look at the picture of rubbish in the Learner's Book and talk in small groups about the different materials they can see and whether these need to be made or not. Assess what learners know already by listening to some discussions then asking learners to tell the whole class about the materials they have been talking about.

Listen for learners who say that paper is wood because it is made from wood or that glass is sand because it is made from sand. Use this topic to explain that the wood, or sand, has been changed into a new material, usually in a factory. So paper is not wood, but it does contain some of the things that make up wood.

2 Materials alphabet game (15 minutes)

Resources: A sheet of paper/small whiteboard

Description: Ask learners to work in pairs or small groups to try to name a material for each letter of the alphabet. Give them up to ten minutes, then count up which group has the most materials and check through their list with the class. Ask the other learners to say whether they agree that each thing in the list is a material.

Look out for learners who list objects in their lists. See the misconceptions section above.

Main teaching ideas

1 Explaining 'natural' and 'made' (15 minutes)

Learning intention: We are going to learn about where materials come from.

We are going to learn which materials are natural and which materials have been made by people.

Resources: Learner's Book

Description: Read to learners about the differences between natural and made materials (Learner's Book Topic 3.1). Then ask 'Who can say what 'natural' means?'. If necessary, explain that natural materials are those that can be found in nature. They are materials that people do not have to make.

Ask learners to talk about other things that can be natural or made. Ask 'How is a swimming pool different from a river?' and 'Some people used to live in caves. How is a cave different from a house?'.

> **Differentiation ideas:** Provide support for learners by showing them a small collection of natural and made materials for example, a twig, a stone, a metal paper clip and a plastic ruler. Help these learners to decide whether these materials are natural or made by asking 'Would you find this in a forest?'.

You could challenge learners with a good understanding of materials by asking 'How is brick (or concrete) different from a rock?'. Bricks and concrete are made by people, but rocks are found in nature.

> **Assessment ideas:** Choose individual learners and ask 'Can you name two or more natural materials? Can you name two or more materials that have been made?'

2 Activity: Natural or made materials? (30 minutes)

Learning intention: We are going to learn about where materials come from.

We are going to learn which materials are natural and which materials have been made by people.

Resources: Learner's Book, paper, an outdoor space, flowerbed or garden (optional), Digital Classroom activity – Natural or made? (optional)

Description: NOTE: In this activity you should avoid explaining where cotton comes from. Cotton will be used as an example in 'Think like a scientist: Finding out where materials come from'.

Ask learners to look at the materials around them in the classroom. Ask learners to point out the different materials they see. For some examples, ask learners whether they know where the material comes from and explain if necessary. Look for an opportunity to show that you are interested in extending your own learning by saying that you don't know where a material comes from, or how it is made, but that you would like to find out. Ask learners 'How can we find out?'. Explain, if necessary, that you could look in a book or use the internet to find a website or video. This leads into Think like a scientist 1. Tell learners that they are going to use books, websites or videos to find out more about where materials come from.

After the discussion, ask learners to draw and label pictures of some of the materials found and where they come from. You could use the picture in the Learner's Book (Topic 3.1, Activity: Natural or made?) to explain how they should record their work.

You could extend this activity by taking learners on a hunt around school so they can see a wider range of materials. A flowerbed or garden would allow learners to see a range of natural materials.

Safety: Warn learners not to touch things that could be dangerous, for example, electrical sockets or plants that sting or have thorns.

> **Digital Classroom:** If you have access to the Digital Classroom component, use the activity 'Natural or made?' with learners. Learners can use the activity to sort labelled pictures of materials into 'natural' or 'made' categories. The i button will explain how to use the activity.

> **Differentiation ideas:** You could challenge some learners by asking them to draw, if they can, more than two pictures for each material to show more of the stages involved in making the material.

For learners who need support, you could make a worksheet where they have to match the picture of a material with a picture of where is comes from.

> **Assessment ideas:** Ask learners to label their pictures with the names of the material and to write whether the materials are natural or made. You can then assess their work when marking it.

3 Think like a scientist: Finding out where materials come from (30–40 minutes)

Learning intention: We are going to use books, videos or the internet to answer questions.

We are going to learn about where materials come from.

We are going to learn which materials are natural and which materials have been made by people.

Resources: Simple non-fiction books, printed text, websites or apps about where materials come from, videos about where materials come from (optional) (there are some excellent videos available from the BBC; search the internet for 'BBC Curious Cat video')

Safety: If learners are using the internet, make sure they only use permitted websites.

Description: Read 'Think like a scientist: Finding out where materials come from' to learners. Ask learners which other materials they would like to ask about. Encourage learners to use the structure 'Where does _____ come from?'. Show learners the resources they will use to find out about other materials and, if appropriate, demonstrate how to use the contents page or index in a book to find information about a chosen material. Use the 'Science skills' section at the back of the Learner's Book. Read, with learners, the part called 'How to stay safe online'. This explains to learners how to use the internet safely.

Ask learners to record their answers using simple flow diagrams like the example given in the Learner's Book.

Look out for learners who think that all factories make materials. Many factories simple change the shape of materials as in the cotton example used in the Learner's Book (see the misconceptions section above).

After the activity, choose learners to use their work to tell the class what they have found out.

> **Differentiation ideas:** For learners who need more support with reading, you could prepare some short simple texts that describe where different materials come from and how they are used that are similar to the text about cotton in the Learner's Book.

More confident readers could use more detailed non-fiction books.

4 Workbook 3.1 (20 minutes)

Learning intention: We are going to learn which materials are natural and which materials have been made by people.

We are going to learn about where materials come from.

We are going to use books, videos or the internet to answer questions.

Resources: Workbook

Description: Learners should answers the questions in the Workbook to identify natural and made materials, match materials to where they come from and to answer questions from an information text.

> **Assessment ideas:** Use the activities in the Workbook to assess whether learners have met the success criteria for this topic.

Plenary ideas

1 Reflection (10 minutes)

Resources: A piece of cotton clothing, for example, a t-shirt, water, a large bowl

Description: Show learners a piece of cotton clothing and ask 'How did we find out if this cotton was natural or made material?'. If necessary, explain to learners that the answer was found by using a book, a video or the internet.

Next ask 'Can the answers to all science questions be found in books? Are there different ways to answer science questions?'. Discuss this with learners. Explain, if necessary, that some science questions can be answered by observation or by testing in an investigation.

Ask 'Is this cotton fabric waterproof? How can we find the answer to that question?'. Discuss learners' responses and explain, if necessary, that you could find out by doing a simple test.

Ask learners to suggest a possible test. They might suggest putting a little water onto the fabric and watching to see if it soaks in, or they might suggest holding the fabric over a bowl and pouring a little water on top to see whether it goes through. You could explain or demonstrate these tests if necessary.

Ask learners 'Could we answer the first question, Is cotton a natural or a made material?, by doing

a test?' Explain to learners, if necessary, that this cannot be answered by testing the material. Explain to learners that different science questions can be answered in different ways.

You could extend this activity by asking learners to suggest other science questions that could be answered using secondary sources and other that could be answered by testing.

2 Let's recycle and reuse (10 minutes)

Resources: A plastic bottle of water, pictures of plastic waste (search the internet for 'plastic waste'), pictures of reused objects, for example, plastic bottles (search the internet for 'upcycling'), pictures of recycling bins

Description: Ask learners 'Why is it good to recycle or reuse materials?'. Discuss their responses and explain, if necessary, that making materials and making objects from materials uses energy and produces waste which is bad for our planet. Show pictures of plastic waste and explain that this is particularly bad as plastic takes hundreds of years to rot away. Explain that much plastic dropped as litter gets into streams and rivers and into the sea where it is damaging habitats of many living things.

Show learners the plastic bottle of water and ask 'What could we do instead of throwing the plastic away when the bottle is empty?'. Discuss learners' answers and explain, if necessary, that refilling the bottle with clean water to use it again is best as it creates no waste. The second best option is recycling the bottle in recycling bins because the plastic will be used again, meaning less new plastic needs to be made.

If appropriate, you could encourage learners to reuse plastic bottles to bring drinking water to school. The bottles should be labelled with the learners' names. You could also re-use objects for different purposes around the classroom, for example, making pen pots out of bottles by removing the top section, or making book storage units out of used cardboard boxes.

> **Assessment ideas:** Ask learners to name other waste materials they have seen dropped as litter. Choose individual learners to say whether the named material is natural or made by people.

You could challenge some learners to explain why it is better for the planet to use natural materials to make things. Learners who understand making materials uses energy may be able to explain that using natural materials uses less energy, which causes less pollution.

This topic has links with how land is used in geography. Learners could use look at photographs and discuss places where natural materials grow or are collected. For example, managed forests, fields that grow crops, quarries, plantations, coal mines, reservoirs and oil rigs.

Homework ideas

Ask learners find out whether they can recycle any of their waste at home. If recycling facilities are available, learners could be asked to make a poster encouraging people to recycle used materials.

Ask learners to draw some materials they find at home, name them and write whether they are natural materials or made materials.

3.2 Properties of materials

LEARNING PLAN

Learning objectives	Learning intention	Success criteria
2Cp.01 Describe a property as a characteristic of a material and understand that materials can have more than one property.	• We are going to learn about the properties of different materials. • We are going to learn that materials have more than one property.	• I can talk about the properties of four or more materials. • I can name two or more properties of some materials.
2TWSp.01 Ask questions about the world around us and talk about how to find answers.	• We are going to ask questions about materials and find answers by observing.	• I can ask a question about a material and show how to find the answer.
2TWSc.01 Sort and group objects, materials and living things based on observations of the similarities and differences between them.	• We are going to put materials into groups using their properties.	• I can use properties to sort materials into groups.

LANGUAGE SUPPORT

The characteristics of materials such as hard, strong and rough are adjectives. Encourage learners to learn and use these new adjectives in their writing.

In this topic learners could write sentences using appropriate quantifiers such as 'most', 'some' and 'all'. Sentences such as 'Most metal is rigid' or 'All fabric is flexible' can be used.

You could ask learners to write simple sentences about different materials that use commas to separate items in a list. For example, 'Metal is hard, shiny, waterproof and rigid'.

absorbent: something that soaks up water and other liquids, not waterproof

characteristic: what a material or a living thing is like, for example, a material could have characteristics of being flexible or rigid, an animal could have characteristics of having two legs or four legs

dull: something that light does not bounce off, not shiny

flexible: something that can bend, squash or twist, not rigid

property/properties: what something is like, for example, smooth and shiny are properties of glass

rigid: something that keeps its shape and is not easy to bend, squash or twist, not flexible

rough: something is bumpy, not flat, not smooth

shiny: something that light bounces off, not dull

smooth: something that is flat, not bumpy, not rough

strong: something that is not easy to break, not weak

Venn diagram: a picture used for sorting with two circles that overlap

weak: something that is easy to break, not strong

Common misconceptions

Misconception	How to identify	How to overcome
Some learners confuse the material properties soft and smooth.	Point out materials that are soft but not smooth such as a sponge or a knitted jumper. Ask 'Is this material smooth?'.	Explain and demonstrate that soft means that the material can be easily squashed but smooth means the material is flat without bumps or holes.
Some learners confuse the material properties hard and strong.	Point out materials that are hard but not strong such as a plastic ruler. Ask 'Is this material hard? Is it strong? Do you think you could break it?'.	Explain and demonstrate that hard means that the material can not be easily squashed but strong means the material is difficult to break.

Starter ideas

1 Getting started (10 minutes)

Resources: Scrap paper or small whiteboards

Description: Ask learners to name some common materials. If appropriate you could remind learners about work done on materials in Stage 1 (see Background Knowledge section). Then ask 'Who can give an example of a property of a material?'. Learners might suggest hard, strong or flexible.

If they cannot think of any properties say 'One property of metal is that it is strong. Properties tell us what materials are like. Can anyone think of another material that is strong?'. Ask each learner to make a list of the properties they can think off on scrap paper or small whiteboards. Then ask them to name a material that has each property they have listed. Learners could work in pairs.

Ask learners to share their ideas with the class and ask other learners to show whether they agree or disagree. Challenge some learners to say why they agree or disagree.

Look out for learners who make incorrect statements such as 'Wood is rough'. Encourage these learners to use appropriate quantifiers such as 'most' or 'some'. You could ask 'Is all wood rough or just some wood?'.

2 Actions for characteristics (15 minutes)

Resources: Learner's Book, Digital Classroom activity: Material characteristics (optional)

Description: Read the section in the Learner's Book that introduces the material properties rigid, flexible, waterproof, absorbent and strong to learners. It also explains that 'characteristic' is another word for 'properties'.

Ask learners to suggest actions they could use to help them remember the words. For example, the word strong could be spoken accompanied with arms held up showing strong muscles, the word flexible combined with fingers linked and forearms waving loosely. Repeat with new actions for other material characteristics.

Write the characteristics on the board and ask learners to demonstrate the actions and say each word as you point to them. Using actions will help learners remember the words.

Look out for learners who find it hard to remember the action for each characteristic because this could indicate that they do not understand the word. Check the understanding of these learners individually in the following activities.

> **Digital Classroom:** If you have access to the Digital Classroom component, use the activity 'Material characteristics' with learners. Learners will see pictures demonstrating characteristic of materials. They have to select the correct word that describes the characteristic. The i button will explain how to use the activity.

Main teaching ideas

1 Think like a scientist 1: Questions about materials (30–40 minutes)

Learning intention: We are going to learn about the properties of different materials.

We are going to learn that materials have more than one property.

We are going to ask questions about materials and find answers by observing.

Resources: Learner's Book, prepared table for results as shown in the Learner's Book, a selection of familiar objects each made of a single material, for example, a rubber balloon, a plastic bag, a metal paper clip, a wooden twig, a piece of writing paper, a piece of cotton string (fabric), a rock, a glass bottle, if learners are going to test whether materials are waterproof/absorbent, then they will need water in beakers, Digital Classroom song – Sort it out (optional)

Practical guidance: Read 'Think like a scientist 1: Questions about materials' in the Learner's Book to learners. Ask learners to suggest other questions they could investigate such as 'Is it waterproof or absorbent?' or 'Is it flexible or rigid?'. Learners can test whether a material is waterproof or absorbent by using a finger to put a drop of water onto the material and observing whether it is absorbed or remains on the surface. You may need to demonstrate this test.

Learners could do a simple test to find out whether a material is flexible or rigid by trying to bend the material.

If learners are going to test whether materials are strong or weak, make it clear to learners whether they are allowed to damage the objects they are using.

Safety: Do not use objects that could break into sharp pieces. Warn learners to be careful with any damaged objects.

> **Digital Classroom:** If you have access to the Digital Classroom component, you can use the song 'Sort it out' with learners. The animation shows materials being sorted into different groups. Teach learners the chorus so they can join in. The i button will explain how to use the song.

> **Differentiation ideas:** Learners who need more support could work in a group guided by the teacher. These learners could all test or observe one material before moving on to the next.

Learners who are better at planning their own tests could work independently or in pairs testing or observing a material in different ways and moving on when they are ready.

Some learners could be challenged to observe whether materials feel warm or feel cold to touch. Materials that 'feel warm' are thermal insulators. Materials that 'feel cold' are thermal conductors.

> **Assessment ideas:** Peer assessment: Ask learners to compare their results with others. If they have different answers for the same material, ask them to test or observe the material again.

2 Think like a scientist 2: Using a Venn diagram for sorting (30 minutes)

Learning intention: We are going to put materials into groups using their properties.

We are going to learn that materials have more than one property.

Resources: Learner's Book, Venn diagrams drawn on paper and labelled, as shown in the Learner's Book; unlabelled Venn diagrams for some learners (see differentiation below), a selection of familiar objects, each made of a single material, for example, a rubber balloon, a plastic bag, a metal paper clip, a wooden twig, a piece of writing paper, a piece of cotton string (fabric), a rock, a glass bottle

Description: Read to learners 'Think like a scientist 2: Using a Venn diagram for sorting' in the Learner's Book. Ask learners to say where in the Venn diagram they think the glass bottle should go. If they are not sure, then ask 'Is the glass bottle shiny? Is it flexible?'.

Choose two material characteristics that are not opposites for this sorting activity, for example, strong/flexible rather than strong/weak. Good characteristics to use include waterproof/flexible, strong/absorbent, smooth/soft.

Show learners the selection of materials they will be using for the activity and the labelled Venn diagram they will use. Ask learners to use what they have learnt about materials to put them into the groups. Make sure learners understand that materials recorded in the Venn diagram crossover must show both of the characteristics used.

Safety: If using glass bottles, warn learners to take care and make sure they are made of strong glass. Do not use objects that could break into sharp pieces.

> **Differentiation ideas:** Learners who find sorting materials difficult could be given a smaller selection objects to sort.

Some learners may be able to choose which two material characteristics to use for this sorting activity. For these learners give them unlabelled Venn diagrams and ask them to write one of their chosen (non-opposite) material characteristic for each circle.

> **Assessment ideas:** Peer assessment Ask learners to have a look at another learner's finished Venn diagrams and talk about whether they agree or disagree with where they have recorded the materials. If they disagree, ask them to explain why.

3 Workbook 3.2 (15–30 minutes)

Learning intention: We are going to learn about the properties of different materials.

We are going to learn that materials have more than one property.

We are going to put materials into groups using their properties.

Resources: Workbook

Description: Learners can use Workbook: Topic 3.2 to identify and sort material characteristics. Learners start by matching materials to characteristics in the Focus activity. The Practice section ask them to sort materials into a Venn diagram. In the Challenge activity, they have to choose the correct properties to complete sentences about materials.

> **Assessment ideas:** Use this activity to assess learners' understanding of the characteristics of materials and their sorting skills.

Plenary ideas

1 Reflection (10 minutes)

Description: Ask learners 'Why is it sometimes better to use a Venn diagram than two different groups?'. Explain, if necessary, than a Venn diagram can show us more information. Items positioned where the two circles cross over are shown to have more than one property. In the case of materials, it shows clearly when a material has both of the characteristics being used.

Show learners some other Venn diagrams that are useful for science and ask learners to suggest things that could go into each part of the diagram. For example:

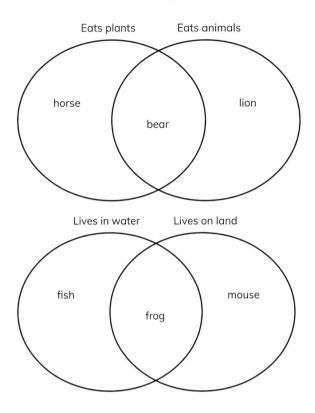

2 Using quantifiers (15 minutes)

Resources: Class whiteboard/blackboard or large sheets of paper.

Description: Write some sentences about material characteristics on the board or on large sheets of paper. For example, Plastic is shiny.

Metal is strong.

Glass is not flexible.

Wood is rough.

Ask learners whether they agree or disagree with each sentence and whether each one could be improved. 'Plastic is shiny' is a good sentence to start with because some plastic is shiny but plenty of plastic is dull.

If learners agree with the sentence, ask them to look closely at plastic objects around the classroom. Ask 'Are they all shiny?'. When a dull plastic object is found, agree with the class that the sentence needs to be changed.

If necessary, display a list of quantifiers on the board for learners to choose from 'most, some, many, no, all'. Change the sentence to 'Some plastic is shiny.' and ask whether learners now agree or disagree. Repeat for the other sentences.

> **Reflection ideas:** This activity demonstrates that scientists should collect a wide range of information before making general conclusions. Describe a scenario to learners 'Umar looks at one piece of shiny plastic and says 'Plastic is shiny'. Ask 'Is this good science?'. Learners may respond by explaining that the sentence is wrong because only some plastic is shiny, but ask them to say what Umar should do before saying what he has found out. Explain, if necessary, that they he observe many types of material before making such general statements. Point out that Umar could say 'Some plastic is shiny'. Explain that when we are talking about what we have found out in science, we need to choose our words very carefully to make sure what we say is correct.

CROSS-CURRICULAR LINKS

This topic could be linked to art and poetry with an activity on creating calligrams. Calligrams are pieces of text where the design and layout of the letters create a picture that represents the meaning of the words. Learners could choose a material characteristic and draw calligrams to illustrate them.

For example,

Homework ideas

Give learners a list of material characteristics and ask them to find an object at home that has each characteristic. Ask learners to draw each object and label it with the materials it is made of.

Ask learners to draw a picture showing an outdoor place and then label things in the picture with material characteristics. For example, a wall could be labelled strong, a leaf could be labelled flexible, soil could be labelled absorbent.

3.3 Using the right material

LEARNING PLAN

Learning objectives	Learning intention	Success criteria
2Cp.02 Explain why materials are chosen for specific purposes on the basis of their properties.	• We are going to find out why a material can be good for making some objects but not others.	• I can say why a material has been used to make an object.
2TWSc.06 Collect and record observations and/or measurements by annotating images and completing simple tables.	• We are going to record our observations in a table.	• I can record observations in a table.

LANGUAGE SUPPORT

This topic develops learners reasoning skills. You could encourage this in learners' spoken and written English by asking them to use the simple connective 'because' to join simple sentences. For

example, 'Windows are made of glass,' and 'Glass is transparent,' can be joined to become 'Windows are made of glass **because** glass is transparent'.

transparent: a material you can see through clearly

Common misconceptions

Misconception	How to identify	How to overcome
Some learners may confuse brightly painted wood or metal with plastic.	Show learners some brightly painted objects made from wood or metal, for example, a painted wooden chair. Ask learners to say what they think the objects are made of.	If possible show learners a scratch on the paint that shows the material beneath. Show learners a painted wooden pencil, but hide both ends in your hands. Ask learners to say what material they think it is. If they say plastic, show the sharp end of the pencil and ask them again. Ask learners to explain why they thought the pencil was made of plastic. Explain, if necessary, that the paint makes a thin layer over the wood that looks a bit like plastic.

Starter ideas

1 What is it made of? (10 minutes)

Resources: A selection of familiar objects each made of a single material, for example, a rubber balloon, a plastic bag, a metal paper

clip, a wooden twig, a piece of writing paper, a piece of cotton string (fabric), a rock, a glass bottle

Description: Line up the objects where the learners can see them and ask them to all say the name of the material when you point to the object. Repeat this, but explain to learners that you are going to see how fast they can name the objects. If they do well, you could put the objects into a different order and repeat the game.

You could extend this game by asking individual learners to try to remember the order of the materials with their eyes closed.

Look out for learners who name the object instead of the material it is made from. Ask these learners to name the materials more slowly so they can think more carefully.

2 Getting started (10 minutes)

Resources: Learner's Book

Description: Read the 'Getting started' section of the Learner's Book (Topic 3.3) to Learners. Ask 'Why are windows made from glass?' then ask learners to talk in small groups about their answers before choosing some learners to tell the class their group's ideas.

If learners talk about being able to see through glass ask 'Does anyone know the science word for 'see-through'?'. Explain, if necessary, that the word 'transparent' is used for something that we can see through clearly. Explain that it is a property of glass and some other materials.

Now ask 'Could a window be made from a different material?' and ask learners again to talk in small groups about their answers before choosing some learners to tell the class their group's ideas.

Learners may suggest plastic, water, ice or diamond. Explain, if necessary, that some plastics are transparent as well as water, ice and some rocks such as diamond. Ask 'Is water a sensible material for a window? What would happen to a window made of water?'. Explain that water is not rigid so it would not make a good window because a material used for a window needs to be transparent and rigid. Explain that windows are sometimes made from transparent plastic, but plastic is not as hard as glass and scratches more easily and these windows become less transparent as they become more scratched.

Some learners may think that all glass is weak. Explain that thin glass is weak, but for glass used in cars and bus windscreens, pieces of thin glass are stuck together in layers to make the glass thicker and stronger.

Main teaching ideas

1 Activity 1: Sensible and silly materials (25 minutes)

Learning intention: We are going to find out why a material can be good for making some objects but not others.

Resources: Learner's Book, Worksheet 3.3A, 3.3B and 3.3C (optional)

Description: Read the text about sensible and silly materials in the Learner's Book (Topic 3.3) with learners. Ask learners to suggest other materials that would be silly to use to make a bike or a table. Learners might suggest that a table or a bike made from rock would be too heavy to move. If made from fabric, they would be too flexible.

Ask learners to draw pictures of an object made of a sensible material and the same object made of a silly material. Learners could use Worksheet 3.3A, 3.3B or 3.3C. Ask learners to explain their reasoning to others by saying what property the chosen material has that makes it either sensible or silly for the object.

For example, metal is a sensible material for a bike because it is strong but rubber is a silly material for a bike because it is flexible.

> **Differentiation ideas:** Learners who need more support could use Worksheet 3.3A. Using this, they only have to name a sensible and silly material for making one object.

Some learners could use Worksheet 3.3C, which challenges them to record their reasoning for each picture by writing what property the chosen material has that makes it either sensible or silly.

> **Assessment ideas:** Assess individual learners by asking them to explain what property the chosen material has that makes it either sensible or silly for the object.

Assess learners who are recording their reasoning after the activity by marking their work.

2 Activity 2: Why is that material useful? (25 minutes)

Learning intention: We are going to find out why a material can be good for making some objects but not others.

We are going to record our observations in a table.

Resources: Learner's Book, objects in the classroom and a prepared table of results as shown in the Learner's Book for each learner, Digital Classroom activity: Why do we use...? (optional)

Description: Read 'Activity 2: Why is that material useful?' in the Learner's Book (Topic 3.3) with learners. Explain to learners that they are going to look at objects in the classroom and record the objects' useful properties in a table of results. Ask learners 'Why is 'waterproof' not written in the table in the Learner's Book?'. Explain, if necessary, that learners do not have to record all the properties of the material, only the useful properties for each object.

Allow learners 10 to 15 minutes to complete their tables of results. You could allow learners to move around the classroom so they can touch objects and observe them closely.

> **Digital Classroom:** If you have access to the Digital Classroom component, use the activity 'Why do we use...?' with learners. Learners have to complete sentences that explain why a material has been used to make the objects pictured. The i button will explain how to use the activity.

> **Differentiation ideas:** You or another adult could lead a group of learners who need support in this activity. The group could all work on the same object at once and share their ideas before recording in the table.

Learners who complete this activity quickly could by challenged to suggest other materials that could be used for making each object.

> **Assessment ideas:** Self/peer assessment

After the activity, show learners a reading book and ask 'What properties of paper are not useful for this book?'. Explain, if necessary, that paper is weak so the book could get torn and it is absorbent so the book could get damaged if it gets wet. Ask learners 'Would you record these properties in your table if you were thinking about a book?'. Remind learners, if necessary, that they should only be recording the useful properties then get learners to look back at their work. You could ask learners to make corrections by crossing out any non-useful properties they have recorded with a coloured pencil.

After the activity, learner's work can be assessed to find out whether they can identify why a material has been used to make a specific object.

3 Workbook 3.3 (30 minutes)

Learning intention: We are going to find out why a material can be good for making some objects but not others.

Resources: Workbook

Description: Learners can use the Focus activity to identify a material used to make an object and a useful property of that material. The Practice section asks them complete a sentence by identifying useful properties from a list. The Challenge activity ask learners to think about the different materials used to make a car.:

> **Assessment ideas:** Use this activity to assess whether learners can correctly identify why a material has been used to make an object.

Plenary ideas

1 A car made of cake! (10 minutes)

Resources: Video of a car made from cake (Search the internet for 'Car cake car advert')

Description: Show learners a video of a car being made from cake and discuss why the materials used are silly. You could ask 'What would happen to a car made from cake?' or 'What would happen if your tried to drive it?' or 'What would happen if it rained?'. Ask learners to talk in small groups about their answers before choosing some learners to tell the class their group's ideas.

> **Assessment ideas:** Ask individual learners to say why cake is not a good material for a specific part of a car by identifying properties that cake does not have. For example, Ask 'Why is cake not a good material to make the windows?'. If necessary, ask 'What properties do windows need that cake does not have?'.

2 Clothes made of metal! (10 minutes)

Resources: Pictures of suits of armour.

Description: Ask learners 'What would clothes made from metal be like to wear?', discuss their answers then ask a learner to pretend to walk while wearing metal clothes. Ask learners to say what properties of metal make it a sensible or silly material for making clothes. Explain, if necessary, the metal is often rigid, but clothes need to be flexible.

Show pictures of suits of armour and ask 'Do these clothes look sensible or silly?'. Explain, if necessary, that a long time ago people wore suits of armour in battle to protect themselves. Explain that the metal has special joints at the knees and elbows so the people wearing the armour could still move.

Homework ideas

Learners could be asked to continue or repeat Activity 2: Why is that material useful? using objects found at home.

Ask learners to draw and label a picture at home of an object made from a silly material.

Topic worksheets

Worksheets 3.3A, 3.3B and 3.3C

In these Worksheets, learners have to draw pictures of objects made of a sensible material and the same object made of a silly material.

Learners who need more support could use Worksheet 3.3A where they only have to name a sensible and silly material for making one object.

The majority of learners should be able to complete Worksheet 3.3B, where learners have to choose the materials and the final object.

Some learners could use Worksheet 3.3C, which challenges them to record their reasoning for each picture by writing what property the chosen material has that makes it either sensible or silly.

3.4 Testing materials

LEARNING PLAN

Learning objectives	Learning intention	Success criteria
2Cp.03 Know that materials can be tested to determine their properties.	• We are going to learn that we can test materials to find out their properties.	• I can test materials to find out their properties.
2TWSp.02 Make predictions about what they think will happen.	• We are going to make predictions.	• I can make a prediction.
2TWSc.03 Take measurements in non-standard units.	• We are going to use bricks or counters to measure.	• I can measure using bricks or counters.
2TWSa.03 Present and interpret results using tables and block graphs.	• We are going to use and make a block graph.	• I can use and make a block graph.

LANGUAGE SUPPORT

This topic requires learners to use many common adjectives in the simple, comparative and superlative forms. These adjectives often use the common suffixes -er and -est.

For example, soft, softer, softest, or strong, stronger, strongest.

However, some of the adjectives used will require the use of the words 'more' and 'less' to create the comparative form and the words 'most' or 'least' to create the superlative form.

For example, waterproof, more waterproof/less waterproof, most waterproof/least waterproof.

These adjectives could be displayed in the classroom in the following format to support learners.

soft	strong	weak	waterproof	flexible
softer	stronger	weaker	more waterproof	less flexible
softest	strongest	weakest	most waterproof	least flexible

Learners can use the Unit 3 Language worksheets to practise spelling some of these adjectives.

block graph: a way of showing results that uses squares or blocks instead of numbers

Common misconceptions

Misconception	How to identify	How to overcome
Most learners will think that fabrics are either waterproof or absorbent. In fact many waterproof fabrics will absorb water if they are wet for long enough.	Talk with learners about waterproof fabrics. Show some pictures or fabric samples and ask them to say which of the waterproof fabrics they think will be the most waterproof. Learners with this misconception may simply state that all the fabrics are waterproof.	Think like a scientist 1: Which fabric is best for an umbrella? will introduce the idea that some fabrics can be more waterproof than others. Testing different waterproof fabrics by leaving drops of water sitting on them for a long time will show that even waterproof fabrics are slightly absorbent.

Starter ideas

1 Getting started (10 minutes)

Resources: Learner's Book

Description: Read the 'Getting started' section of the Learner's Book, Topic 3.4 with learners. Ask learners to look at the fabric of their clothes and to say whether they think it is waterproof. Then ask learners to talk in pairs or small groups about how they could find out. Choose learners to share their group's ideas and discuss them with the class.

Learners may suggest putting water on the fabrics to find out what happens. Some learners may talk about past experience, for example, 'I split water on my jumper and it was not waterproof'. Ask these learners to describe what happened to the fabric and to explain how they could see that the fabric was not waterproof. If necessary, ask 'What would have happened differently if the fabric was waterproof?'.

Explain to learners that when you do not know the properties of a material, one way to find out is to test the material.

Ask learners to indicate whether they agree or disagree with the statement 'Waterproof fabrics never absorb water'. Choose learners to say why they agree or disagree. Learners who agree with the statement do not understand than many waterproof fabrics do absorb water when they are wet for a long time.

2 Testing cushions (10 minutes)

Resources: Learner's Book, sticky notes, class whiteboard/blackboard,

Description: Read the section in the Learner's Book about testing the softness of cushions with learners. You could demonstrate the technique shown to measure the softness using a real cushion.

Show learners the block graph and ask them to say which were the softest and hardest cushions. Then ask 'How many more bricks were needed for the green cushion than the red cushion?' and 'How many fewer bricks were need for the blue cushion than the red cushion?'.

Draw axes on the class whiteboard/blackboard then use sticky notes to recreate the block graph shown in the Learner's Book. Ask learners 'Who can put these sticky notes on the board to show how soft the green cushion was?'. Choose a learner to do this. Then ask 'Why do we need five sticky notes?'. Explain, if necessary, that if learners look at the pictures in the Learner's Book, they can see that the green cushion had five bricks. Repeat this for the other two cushions.

Look out for learners who think that the blue cushion was the softest. This could be because the blue cushion's block graph is smaller, making it look like the cushion has been squashed more than the others. Explain that the graph shows the number of bricks used to measure the dent in the cushion, so the more the cushion squashed, the more bricks were needed. "If necessary read, with learners, the 'Science skills' section at the back of the Learner's Book. Read the part called 'How to draw a block graph', this uses step by step instructions to show learners the process of drawing a block graph."

Main teaching ideas

1 Think like a scientist 1: Which fabric is best for an umbrella? (15–20 minutes)

Learning intention: We are going to learn that we can test materials to find out their properties.

We are going to make predictions.

Resources: Learner's Book, for each group: a cup of water and samples of two or more different fabrics, including one that is waterproof and one that is absorbent, magnifying glasses (optional), Worksheet 3.4A, 3.4B or 3.4C

Description: Read 'Think like a scientist 1: Which fabric is best for an umbrella?' with learners. Show learners the fabrics they will be using and ask them to predict which fabric will be most waterproof.

Show learners how to put a drop of water onto the fabric by dipping a finger into the water then shaking it above the fabric so that a drop falls onto the fabric. Explain that learners should not touch the fabric with their finger because this could cause the water to be absorbed more quickly.

Explain to learners that they need to observe closely and wait to see what happens. Tell learners to count slowly to twenty each time they observe, because leaving the water on one fabric much longer than the others would make the comparison unfair. Learners could use magnifying glasses to observe the water drop and the fabric more closely.

Learners could record their observations by drawing and labelling the water drops and the fabrics. After the activity, ask learners to say whether their predictions were correct.

Safety: Tell learners not to drink the water.

Learners could use Worksheets 3.4A, 3.4B or 3.4C to draw a block graph based on this investigation.

> **Differentiation ideas:** Learners who need support could work in a guided group with yourself or another adult.

Some learners could be challenged to compare a wider range of fabrics. They might find this easier if several learners work together to each place a drop of water on a different fabric at the same time. The slower the water is absorbed, the more waterproof the fabric is.

> **Assessment ideas:** Ask learners to record their predictions at the start of this activity so these can be assessed when marking their work.

2 Workbook 3.4 (15 minutes)

Learning intention: We are going to use bricks or counters to measure.

We are going to use and make a block graph.

Resources: Workbook

Description: The Focus activity of the workbook asks learners to use a set of results to draw a block graph. In the Practice and Challenge sections, learners have to use the results or the block graph to answer questions.

> **Assessment ideas:** You can assess whether learners have drawn the block graph correctly and can use a block graph to answer questions by marking their work.

3 Think like a scientist 2: Which paper makes the strongest bag? (30 minutes)

Learning intention: We are going to make predictions.

We are going to use bricks or counters to measure.

We are going to use and make a block graph.

Resources: Learner's Book, each pair or group will need: a prepared table of results with a column for the type of paper, a column for their predictions and a column for the number of bricks, prepared axes for drawing the block graph, three small strips of different types of paper, each with a hole punched in one end (use paper of different colours to make them easy to identify or label the different samples A, B and C), a paper clip, a small thin rubber band, a pencil and some counters or counting bricks

Description: Read 'Think like a scientist 2: Which paper makes the strongest bag?' with learners. This explains how to complete this investigation. Show learners the different types of paper they are going to test and ask learners to predict which will be the strongest. Challenge some learners to give reasons for their predictions. Demonstrate for learners how to measure the length of the rubber band using the counters or counting bricks they will be using. Learners should record their predictions in the prepared table.

Safety: Make sure learners hold the pencil at both ends to pull on the rubber band. This will stop the paperclip from hitting anything else when the paper tears.

Give learners time to work in pairs or small groups to test each type of paper and record their results in the table, then ask learners to peer assess by comparing their results with others. Ask 'Which paper is the strongest?'. If learners do not agree, then ask them to say why they might have different results. Learners might suggest that they might not have held the pencil in the right place or counted the bricks correctly. If necessary, ask some groups of learners to check some of their measurements.

Note: It is not necessary for all groups to get the same measurements because there may be some differences in the rubber bands used, but all groups

should agree on which paper is strongest and which is weakest. If necessary, repeat the investigation as a demonstration for the whole class for a definitive set of results.

After the investigation, ask learners to use their results to draw a block graph using prepared axes. Here you could re-read, with learners, the 'Science skills' section at the back of the Learner's Book. The part called 'How to draw a block graph' uses step by step instructions to show learners the process of drawing a block graph. When complete, show some examples of these to the class and ask learners to explain what they show. Finish the activity by asking learners 'Which paper would make the strongest bag?'.

> **Differentiation ideas:** You or another adult could work with a group of learners who need more support in this activity. The learners should do the practical work, but extra guidance can be given if learners are not measuring accurately or keeping the test fair.

Learners who need more support could be paired with other learners who can help them with the measuring and in completing the investigation fairly.

Some learners could be challenged to create their block graph without using the prepared axes. These learners could use squared paper.

> **Assessment ideas:** Observe learners while they are working to assess the accuracy of their measuring. The block graphs can be assessed when you mark their work.

Plenary ideas

1 Reflection (5 minutes)

Description: Talk with learners about the measuring they did in Think like a scientist 2 Which paper makes the strongest bag?.

Say to learners 'It was sometimes hard to measure the rubber band because it moves as soon as the paper tears'. Then ask 'Who found the rubber band hard to measure sometimes? What did you do if you were not sure how many bricks long it was?'. Discuss learners' ideas. These might include holding the rubber band closer to the bricks or stretching it more slowly. Say 'So you measured again in a different way'. Explain that a good scientist will always go back and measure again if they are not sure that their measurement is correct.

2 Safety testing (10 minutes)

Resources: A toy with a safety mark printed on it, photos or video of people testing the safety of everyday objects for example, vehicle crash tests (search the internet for 'Safety testing toys/chairs/cars'), you will find photographs of furniture being safety tested on the websites of many large furniture retailers

Description: Show learners a toy and ask 'Is this toy safe for children?'. Discuss learners' ideas then show them the safety mark and explain that most toys, chairs, cars and other everyday things have to be tested to make sure they are safe before they are sold. Show pictures of people doing safety testing and say 'These people are doing almost the same work as you have done in this topic. They have to test things by measuring carefully and then show people what they have found out'.

CROSS-CURRICULAR LINKS

Measuring using non-standard measures is in the maths curriculum at Stage 2. There are many opportunities for learners to practise this skill in this unit. Measurements can be made more accurate by using smaller counters or counting bricks. Most learners will be able to measure to the nearest whole counter or brick. Some learners may be able to measure to the nearest half counter or brick.

Understanding that materials need to be tested before making things is an important concept in design technology. After completing 'Think like a scientist 2: Which paper makes the strongest bag?', learners could go on to make a paper bag. A simple template could be copied onto the strongest paper from the test and learners could cut, fold and glue the template to make a bag. Holes could be punched in the bag and string used for the handles.

Homework ideas

You could ask learners to test the softness of cushions found at home using the technique shown in the Learner's Book. You could give them squared paper and ask them to draw a block graph of the results.

Give learners a completed table of results and prepared axes or squared paper and ask them to draw a block graph of the results.

Topic worksheets

Worksheets 3.4A, 3.4B and 3.4C

Worksheet 3.4A asks learners to draw a block graph to show the results for which fabric let through the most water.

Worksheet 3.4B asks learners to do the same exercise but the number of blocks they need to count is higher.

Worksheet 3.4C challenges learners to draw the block graph and complete the horizontal axis. They also need to answer questions on the results of the investigation.

3.5 Changing materials

LEARNING PLAN

Learning objectives	Learning intention	Success criteria
2Cc.01 Know that some changes can turn a material into a different material.	• We are going to find out how to change some materials.	• I can describe how some materials can be changed.
2TWSp.01 Ask questions about the world around us and talk about how to find answers.	• We are going to ask questions and talk about how to find out the answers.	• I can ask a question and talk about how to find out the answer.
2TWSc.06 Collect and record observations and/or measurements by annotating images and completing simple tables.	• We are going to make labelled diagrams.	• I can draw and label a diagram.
2TWSm.03 Describe the difference between a diagram and a picture.	• We are going to learn how a diagram is different to a picture.	• I can say how a diagram is different to a picture.

LANGUAGE SUPPORT

You could use this topic to explore different types of sentences; statements, commands and questions.

Learners will ask their own questions in Think like a scientist 2 Can you stop peeled fruit going brown? Use this opportunity to explain that questions are different from statements as they ask for information and need a question mark.

Changing materials provides an opportunity for learners to write simple commands that start with an imperative verb.

Here are some examples. Heat chocolate to make it melt. Heat bread to make it into toast. Cool water to make ice.

information: facts about something

liquid: a material that can flow and be poured, for example, water is a liquid

melt: to change from solid to liquid

mixture: something that is made by putting different materials together

solid: a material that keeps its shape and does not flow

Common misconceptions

Misconception	How to identify	How to overcome
Some learners may confuse changing a material with changing an object made of that material.	Show learners a piece of paper and demonstrate that it is very flexible. Then roll it into a tube and show that it has become more rigid. Ask 'Has the material changed or the object?'. Any learners who say that the material has changed may have this misconception.	Explain that the properties of the material have not changed but the properties of the object made from that material have changed. Unroll the paper and demonstrate that the paper is still flexible.

Starter ideas

1 Getting started (10 minutes)

Resources: Learner's Book

Description: Read with learners the 'Getting started' section of the Learner's Book which shows a wooden match burning. Ask learners to describe the properties of wood before it is burnt and the properties of the new material after it is burnt. Ask learners to talk in pairs about other changes to materials they know about and to draw these on small whiteboards or sheets of paper. Choose learners to show their pictures to the class and describe the changes.

Learners might talk about changes that are reversible, such as water freezing to make ice, or boiling to make steam or ice cream melting, or they may talk about changes where new materials are made, such as wood being changed into paper or oil being changed into plastic.

Look out for learners who talk about changing the shape of objects, for example, a piece of wood can be made more flexible by making it thinner. Explain to these learners that these changes do affect the properties of the object, but not the properties of the material.

2 Changes in the kitchen (10 minutes)

Description: Explain to learners that when we cook food, we often change the materials. Give an example such as putting rice in boiling water to make it softer. Ask learners to talk in pairs or small groups about other changes to materials they have seen in the kitchen. Choose some learners to share their group's ideas with the class.

Learners may talk about changes that make new materials, such as making bread into toast or baking bread dough, or they might talk about changes that are reversible, such as water freezing or boiling or ice cream melting.

Look out for learners who talk about changes to objects, for example, opening a plastic wrapper or a metal can. Explain to these learners that these changes do affect the object but not the properties of the material.

Here you could use the 'Science skills' section at the back of the Learner's Book. Read, with learners, the part called 'How to stay safe in the kitchen'. This shows several dangers found in a kitchen. Talk with learners about how they can stay safe in a kitchen. Explain that they should only cook when they are helping an adult, they should keep away from sharp knives and keep water away from electrical appliances.

Main teaching ideas

1 Solids and liquids (10–30 minutes)

Learning intention: We are going to find out how to change some materials.

Resources: Learner's Book, some examples of solids for example, some paper, a plastic ruler, some examples of liquids for example, a glass of water, a bottle of washing up liquid. Workbook: Topic 3.5, video of glass, metal or rock melting (search the internet for 'glass blowing', 'melting metal' or 'lava flow') (optional), hot plate, pan, two eggs (optional), Digital Classroom Science investigators video: The effect of heating different materials? (optional)

Description: Read the section in the Learner's Book about making a cake with learners. If appropriate for your learners, explain that solids are materials that keep their shape and liquids are materials that change shape when you put them in different containers. Show some examples of solid and liquid materials.

Say to learners 'We have seen that chocolate melts. What other materials melt?'. Discuss their answers. Learners might talk about ice, snow, ice cream or butter melting. Some learners may know that glass, metal and rock can melt when they get very hot. (You could show a video of glass, metal or rock melting at this point.)

Explain to learners that heating solids to make them melt is a change that can be reversed. When the solids cool down again, they will turn back into a solid. The solid and the liquid are the same material, but with different properties.

Explain that when liquid egg is heated, it changes into a new material that is solid and it will not change back. This is a different type of change. (You could demonstrate how a boiled or fried egg is different from a raw egg.)

Learners can complete Workbook: Topic 3.5. The Focus activity ask learners to circle five materials being changed in a picture. In the Practice exercise, learners have to identify solids and liquids, and in the Challenge section they have to use key words from this topic to complete simple sentences.

> Digital Classroom: If you have access to the Digital Classroom component, show the Science Investigators video 'The effect of heating different materials'. The video explores what learners know about how different materials change when they are heated. The i button will explain how to use the video.

> Assessment ideas: Ask learners to draw on a small whiteboard or on sheets of paper how some different materials can be changed. While they do this, assess individual learners by asking them to tell you about how their changes happen. Then ask learners to tell a classmate how their changes happen. Assess learners by observing their discussions.

2 Think like a scientist 1: Observing toast (30 minutes)

Learning intention: We are going to find out how to change some materials.

We are going to make labelled diagrams.

We are going to learn how pictures and diagrams are different.

Resources: Learner's Book, some bread, magnifying glasses and a toaster or grill

Safety: Learners should not use the toaster or grill. Talk with learners about how these get very hot and should only be used at home with adult supervision.

Do not allow learners to taste the bread or toast unless the preparation follows appropriate food handling procedures. Check allergy information on packaging and consider known allergies of the learners.

Description: Read 'Think like a scientist 1: Observing toast' with learners. This explains the difference between a diagram and a picture and how to do the investigation.

Ask learners to observe some bread. They could use magnifying glasses if available. Learners can record their observations in a diagram. Encourage learners to draw and label small details by asking the following questions. Are the pieces all the same colour? Are all the holes the same size? Does the bread look rough or smooth? Does it feel rough or smooth? Does it feel hard or soft?

If possible, show a good example of a learner's diagram to the class to make it clearer to learners what you want them to achieve.

Now put the bread in the toaster or grill and explain to learners that the bread is being heated. You could toast some bread so it begins to turn brown and toast some other pieces until they are slightly burnt. Remove the toasted bread and let it cool before allowing learners to observe again. Ask 'How has the bread changed? What is different now? How does it feel?'. Learners should now make further detailed diagrams of the toasted bread.

Explain that some of the bread has now been changed by the heat into a new material. This new material is harder, less flexible and a darker brown or black in colour.

Learners could finish the following simple sentence to explain how the bread was changed into a new material. 'We changed the bread into a new material by ... (heating it/making it hot/putting it in the toaster.)'

> Differentiation ideas: Learners who need more support with making observations could work in pairs with other learners in this activity. These learners could talk about their observations in pairs or with the whole class before drawing their diagrams.

Some learners could be challenged to write a short paragraph describing how the bread was changed into a new material and what it was like before and after heating.

> Assessment ideas: While learners are drawing their diagrams ask individual learners to say how their diagram is different from a picture.

You can assess whether learners can describe how a material can be changed and assess their diagrams by marking their work.

3 Think like a scientist 2: Can you stop peeled fruit going brown? (60 minutes)

Learning intention: We are going to find out how to change some materials.

We are going to ask questions and talk about how to find out the answers.

We are going to make labelled diagrams.

Resources: Learner's Book, two or three apples, a knife and a chopping board, a cup for each learner and a selection of liquids (some water, some salty water, some lemon juice or white vinegar), other clear fizzy drinks such as sparkling water, lemonade (optional)

Description: Note: This activity also works with sliced banana, but banana takes much longer to go brown. If using banana, leave the banana slices in the liquids overnight before comparing with the banana slices left in the air.

Safety: Learners should not taste the fruit unless the preparation follows appropriate food handling procedures. Consider known allergies of the learners.

Description: Read 'Think like a scientist 2: Can you stop peeled fruit going brown?' with learners which explains how to do the investigation. Cut a slice of apple to demonstrate to learners that when it is left in air it will begin to go brown in only a few minutes. Explain that this is because the air makes the apple change into a new material.

Ask learners to suggest how they might stop a slice of apple from going brown. If necessary, ask 'Do you think it would go brown in we put it in water?'. Discuss learners' predictions. Challenge some learners to say why they think the apple would or would not go brown in water.

Remind learners of the meaning of the word 'liquid'. Say 'Water is a liquid. What other liquids might stop the apple going brown?'. Show learners the selection of liquids. Explain that you are going to cut a slice of apple for each learner and one extra slice that you are going to leave in air. Ask learners to choose the liquid they want to investigate and ask a question 'Will (the liquid) stop my apple from going brown?'. Ask learners to record their question and draw a diagram of their planned investigation. Tell them to draw the apple left in air and their own slice of apple in the liquid they have chosen. Learners can peer assess by looking at the questions and diagrams of others and telling them whether their planned investigation will answer their question.

Learners can now pour some of the liquid they want to investigate into their cup. When all learners have done this, cut a slice of apple for each learner to put in their liquid and one slice to be left in the air. Leave the apple slices in the liquids for ten to fifteen minutes, then allow learners to compare their apple slice with the one left in the air. Learners should draw another diagram to show whether the slices have changed or not.

Talk about the results with the class. Ask 'Which liquids stopped the apple from going brown?'. Explain to learners that there is a material in air that makes apple turn brown. Some liquids stop this material getting to the apple so the colour of the apple does not change.

> **Differentiation ideas:** You, or another adult, could work with a small group of learners who need more support with Thinking and Working Scientifically activities. Help these learners to plan their investigation and draw their diagrams by modelling these for them. Alternatively, these learners could work in pairs with learners who are more confident.

Learners could be challenged to make a list of other foods that change when they are left in the air and to describe how they change. For example, bread becomes hard and rigid when it is left out in the air, whereas biscuits become soft when left out in the air.

> **Assessment ideas:** You can assess whether learners can identify how to find out the answers to scientific questions by observing them while they are assessing each others' questions and diagrams.

Plenary ideas

1 Reflection (5 minutes)

Resources: Learner's Book

Description: Show learners the diagram and the picture of bread in the Learner's Book. Ask learners 'How are these different?'.

Ask the reflection questions 'Why is a diagram often more useful than a picture? How does a diagram help you to learn?'

Discuss learners' answers and explain, if necessary, that a diagram helps you to learn by showing you which things are important. Say 'A diagram does not show the things that we don't need to know like who is holding the toast or what colour the plate is.'

> **Assessment ideas:** Choose individual learners to explain how pictures and diagrams are different.

2 Natural and made materials (10 minutes)

Resources: Learner's Book

Description: Show learners Topic 3.1 Natural and made materials in the Learner's Book. Explain that materials that are made start as natural materials. Give one example mentioned in the book. For example, plastic is made from oil. Explain that oil has to be changed into a new material to make plastic. Ask learners to find other examples in the Learner's Book. Possible answers are that the solid rubber we use starts as liquid rubber, wood is changed to make paper and sand is changed to make glass.

> **Assessment ideas:** Use this activity to assess whether learners can describe materials that are changed to make others.

CROSS-CURRICULAR LINKS

There are cross-curricular links with design technology and the life skills subject of cooking. Learners could be involved in a project where they design and make bread or simple biscuits or cakes. Chocolate crispy cakes made from melted chocolate and puffed rice cereal are simple to make with learners. Making them provides an effective demonstration of the material changes in chocolate.

Homework ideas

Ask learners to observe cooking at home and to draw labelled diagrams of the changes to materials that they see.

Ask learners to draw a diagram of their favourite toy at home, labelling it to show some of the important properties, for example, soft fur or smooth wheels. They could also draw a picture of their favourite toy to show the differences between a picture and a diagram.

PROJECT: MATERIALS CAN DAMAGE THE EARTH

2SIC.04 Talk about how science helps us understand our effect on the world around us.

Read the Unit 3 Project in the Learner's Book with learners. Talk with learners about how buying and using recycled paper helps the environment by reducing deforestation. Explain how recycling and disposing of waste plastic correctly can prevent plastic pollution.

For more information on looking after the environment, learners could watch videos and read simple non-fiction books. Talk with learners about other ways that we can help to look after the environment that they know about or have found out about.

Some ways in which learners can help to look after the environment, like opportunities for recycling, will vary in different countries. You could find out about any local recycling facilities. Other ways, such as switching off lights to save electricity, apply everywhere.

Show learners the poster in the Learner's Book and ask learners to make their own poster telling others how to look after the planet. You could give them a poster template to work on.

3 Getting materials right

Project: Materials can damage the Earth

We know that paper is made from wood. Trees are cut down to make paper. This is bad for forests and for the animals and plants that live in forest habitats.

But we can recycle used paper to make new paper. This saves trees.

We know that plastic is made from oil. Oil comes from underground. Getting the oil out causes pollution. Used plastic is often dropped as litter. There is now lots of plastic pollution in our rivers and in the sea.

But we can recycle used plastic to make new plastic. This mean less pollution.

>4 Humans and animals grow

Unit plan

Topic	Approximate number of learning hours	Outline of learning content	Resources
4.1 Comparing animals	2	Observing differences in how animals look, asking scientific questions, using secondary information sources and drawing block graphs.	**Learner's Book:** Think like a scientist 1: Asking questions about animals Think like a scientist 2: How many legs? **Workbook:** Topic 4.1 **Teacher's Resource:** ⬇ Worksheet 4.1A, 4.1B, 4.1C **Digital Classroom:** Activity – What is similar? What is different?
4.2 Growing	3	Observing how animals grow.	**Learner's Book:** Activity 1: How do baby animals change? Activity 2: A younger you Think like a scientist: Measuring height **Workbook:** Topic 4.2 **Teacher's Resource:** ⬇ Worksheets 4.2A, 4.2B, 4.2C **Digital Classroom:** Activity – Adults and babies
4.3 Inheriting characteristics	2	Finding out about the observable characteristics that animals, including humans, inherit from their parents. Observing and sorting fingerprints.	**Learner's Book:** Activity: How are you different? Think like a scientist: Sorting fingerprints **Workbook:** Topic 4.3 **Digital Classroom:** Video – Similar characteristics

Topic	Approximate number of learning hours	Outline of learning content	Resources
4.4 Keeping healthy	3	Finding out about diet, washing and exercise as ways to keep healthy, and learning about what happens when we are ill. Sorting food into groups and investigating the effects of exercise.	**Learner's Book:** Activity: Sorting food Think like a scientist: What happens when we exercise? **Workbook:** Topic 4.4 **Teacher's resource:** ⬇ Worksheets 4.4A, 4.4B, 4.4C **Digital Classroom:** Activity – Healthy food Animation – Keeping healthy
4.5 Teeth	2.5	Learning how to look after teeth. Observing and making a model of the different types of teeth.	**Learner's Book:** Think like a scientist 1: What does sugar do to teeth? Think like a scientist 2: Making model teeth. **Workbook:** Topic 4.5 **Teacher's Resource:** ⬇ Worksheets 4.5A, 4.5B, 4.5C **Digital Classroom:** Activity – Healthy for teeth or not?

Across Unit resources

Learner's Book:

Project: People who use science

Check your progress quiz

Teacher's Resource:

⬇ Language worksheets 1 and 2

⬇ Diagnostic check

Digital Classroom:

⬇ End-of-unit quiz

BACKGROUND KNOWLEDGE

Animals are classified as vertebrates (animals with bones) and invertebrates (animals without bones). The five types of vertebrates are fish, reptiles, mammals, birds and amphibians. Invertebrates include insects, spiders, centipedes, millipedes, worms and molluscs like snails and slugs.

All animals produce young. The young grow into adults who can themselves produce young. Both adult parents pass on some of their characteristic to their young. We say the young inherit these characteristics. An animal's characteristics are determined by a complex chemical structure in cells called DNA. A baby animal's DNA is unique as it is a combination of half of the DNA from the father and half from the mother. This unit focusses on how inherited characteristics affect an animal's appearance, but environmental factors such as climate, diet and accidents can also make a difference to how animals look.

Animals need to eat the correct amount of the correct sort of food to stay healthy. For humans, fruit and vegetables are healthy because they contain fibre, minerals and vitamins, but other foods are less healthy, for example, high sugar

foods. Eating too many unhealthy foods can lead to tooth decay and obesity. Based on scientific evidence, the World Health Organization recommends eating a minimum of 400 g of fruit and vegetables every day. Average consumption around the world is much lower and many governments run campaigns to encourage people to eat five (or more) portions of fruit and vegetables every day.

When discussing diet with learners, be aware that they only have limited control over what they eat. Be aware that some learners may have an unhealthy diet and may be sensitive about this. However, it is perhaps even more important that these learners learn what is healthy. Make it clear to learners that what they drink is just as important as what they eat. Many sugary drinks are marketed at younger children and some claim to be healthy!

Healthy eating is only one part of being healthy. Getting enough exercise, drinking enough water, getting enough sleep and some time to relax are other important factors.

TEACHING SKILLS FOCUS

Language awareness
Develop vocabulary

Learners will already have some vocabulary linked to this topic, for example, about food. As you teach this unit, check that learners understand terms like diet (your diet is what you eat, not a special set of foods chosen to reduce weight). As you introduce new ideas and terms, make pronunciation, meaning and use very clear, for example, this is how we pronounce car-bo-hy-drate, it means …, here is a sentence with it in…

Active learning
Use learners' interest

Many learners will have a lot to say and suggest in relation to health and hygiene because they are likely to have heard quite a lot about it. Use their interest to drive their discussion. For example,

'Does anyone want to tell us about a time when they broke a bone? What happened?'.

Use artefacts to develop explanations

Much of this topic is well-illustrated by things in the home, for example, foods, soaps, toothbrushes, etc. Learners will be familiar with these. They may know what something is and that it is good for you or not, but they may not know why. For example, why is tooth brushing so good for teeth? Why is it important to care for your first teeth?

Use and make models

As this topic includes the study of body parts, you may need to use posters and models if your school has them. If your school has Grade 7 upwards, they may have models of body parts. If not, ask your learners to make models with modelling materials, for example, teeth, and label and write about them.

CONTINUED

Cross curricular learning

Health and hygiene can be linked to personal and social education as well as other subjects, for example, grouping different foods makes use of mathematics skills. In subjects like history and geography, learners can compare their personal diet with those of others around the world and in history.

4.1 Comparing animals

LEARNING PLAN

Learning objectives	Learning intention	Success criteria
2Bs.01 Compare how animals, including humans, are similar and different in their external body parts and skin covering.	• We are going to find out how animals look similar and different.	• I can say how animals look similar and different.
2TWSp.01 Ask questions about the world around us and talk about how to find answers.	• We are going to ask our own questions about animals.	• I can ask my own questions about animals.
2TWSc.05 Use a given secondary information source to find an answer to a question.	• We are going to use books, videos or the internet to answer questions.	• I can use a book, video or the internet to answer questions.
2TWSa.03 Present and interpret results using tables and block graphs.	• We are going to use and make block graphs.	• I can use and make a block graph.

LANGUAGE SUPPORT

Learners will need to use many nouns in this unit, including the names of animals and the names of human and animal body parts. Learners could help to make a class vocabulary display by drawing and labelling different animals.

Learners can use the Unit 4 Language worksheets to practise some of the key words in this unit.

Learners will ask questions in this topic. Help learners to identify questions in text by showing them how to find question marks. Learners could follow the following sentence structure for their own questions *Do _____ have _____?* For example, *do birds have hair?* or *do penguins have wings?*

CONTINUED

bird: an animal with feathers and wings, most birds can fly

feathers: feathers cover the skins of birds and help them to fly

fur: soft hair that covers the skin of some animals

human: a person

mammal: an animal that has hair or fur and has live babies instead of laying eggs

Common misconceptions

Misconception	How to identify	How to overcome
Many learners may think that a human is not an animal.	Read the section in the Learner's Book about mammals and ask 'Did you know that a human is an animal?'.	Explain to learners that, in everyday life, the word 'animal' is not usually used to describe a human but science tells us that humans are a kind of mammal. Explain that the scientific meaning of the word 'animal' does include humans. Explain that we are very different from all other animals and very special because of our brains. Note: Some learners may find this difficult to accept due to their religious beliefs. Be sensitive to this point of view and emphasise that we are very different from other animals and very special.

Starter ideas

1 Getting started (10 minutes)

Resources: Learner's Book

Description: Read the 'Getting started' section in the Learner's Book which shows photos of different animals.

Ask learners to talk with a partner or in a small group to say how the animals look different. Choose learners to tell the class about their group's ideas then ask them to talk about how the animals are similar and choose different learners to share their ideas with the class. Learners might talk about body shape, colour, body parts or body covering such as feathers, fur, etc.

Learners may talk about how the animals behave, where they live, what they eat, etc. This topic is about how animals look, so encourage these learners to concentrate on the animals' bodies and their skin covering.

Check that learners realise that humans are mammals and are therefore animals.

2 Animals at home (10 minutes)

Resources: Photos of animals that learners might keep at home such as cats, goldfish, chickens, birds etc. (optional)

Description: Ask learners to tell the class about any animals they keep at home. Show pictures of some of these animal if possible. Ask learners to talk in small groups about the animals that have been named. Ask 'How are these animals different?' and 'Are any of these animals similar? How are they similar?'. If necessary, prompt learners with questions about the number of eyes the animals have, or the number of legs, skin covering, etc. Choose learners to share their groups' ideas with the class.

Check that learners realise that humans are mammals and are therefore animals.

Main teaching ideas

1 Mammals and birds (25 minutes)

Learning intention: We are going to find out how animals look similar and different.

Resources: Learner's Book, Worksheets 4.1A, 4.1B and 4.1C

Description: Read the section in the Learner's Book that explains about similarities and differences in mammals and birds. Talk with learners about their answers to the questions in the Learner's Book.

Make sure learners give specific examples in their answers. If a learner says that two animals look different because they have different bodies ask them 'How do their bodies look different?'.

Ask learners to complete Worksheet 4.1A, 4.1B or 4.1C, which ask them to identify similarities and differences in different animals.

> **Differentiation ideas:** Learners who need more language support could use Worksheet 4.1A. Some learners could be challenged to use Worksheet 4.1C, which asks learners to write sentences to explain the similarities and differences.

> **Assessment ideas:** While learners are using the worksheets, work with a group of learners to assess whether they can describe how animals look similar and different. Other learners can be assessed by marking their work.

2 Think like a scientist 1: Asking questions about animals (45 minutes)

Learning intention: We are going to ask our own questions about animals.

We are going to use books, videos or the internet to answer questions.

Resources: Learner's Book, books about animals and/or access to the internet for learners (search for 'animal websites for kids'), prepared worksheet, small whiteboards or sticky notes, Digital Classroom activity: What is similar? What is different? (optional)

Description: Read 'Think like a scientist 1: Asking questions about animals' with learners. This shows an example question asked by a learner and how it could be answered. Show learners the books that they are going to use or explain that they are going to use the internet to find answers (or both). Ask learners what questions they would like to ask about animals. Write

a couple of these that use the sentence structure 'Do _____ have _____?' on the board.

Now ask learners to write their own questions about animals using this sentence structure. You could prepare a worksheet that learners could use to record their questions and answers, or learners could use sticky notes or small whiteboards.

Show learners how to look for the answers to their questions and explain that, if the answer is not in the books, then they can ask a different question.

> **Digital Classroom:** If you have access to the Digital Classroom component, use the activity 'What is similar? What is different?' with learners. Learners can use this activity to compare how animals are similar and different. The i button will explain how to use the activity.

> **Practical guidance:** If learners are going to use the internet, you should identify a small selection of age appropriate, learner friendly websites that they can use. Make sure learners are aware of your school's rules for safe internet use.

Use the 'Science skills' section at the back of the Learner's Book. Read, with learners, the section called 'How to stay safe online'. This explains to learners how to use the internet safely.

If using books, show learners how to use the contents or index to look for the name of their animal or the body part they are asking about, for example, wings.

> **Differentiation ideas:** Learners should be given books that are appropriate for their reading level if possible.

> **Assessment ideas:** During the activity, ask learners to read you their question and explain how they are finding the answer. Remember, learners only need to ask a question and talk about how to find the answers. It does not matter if they cannot find the answer to their question.

3 Think like a scientist 2: How many legs? (45 minutes)

Learning intention: We are going to find out how animals look similar and different.

We are going to use and make block graphs.

Resources: Learner's Book, magnifying glasses, an outdoor area where learners can look for small animals, or a prepared worksheet with pictures of small animals, prepared tally charts for learners, prepared block graph for learners, a clear container with lid, (optional), enlarged photographs of small animals (optional)

Description: Read the section in the Learner's Book about looking for and observing small animals with learners. Explain that the question 'How many legs do very small animals have?' can be answered by doing an investigation. Ask learners to say why it would be difficult to do an investigation to answer the earlier question 'Do elephants have hair?'. Explain, if necessary, that you would need to look closely at a real elephant to investigate that question and most people do not have a real elephant to look at.

Show learners the block graph in the Learner's Book. Talk with them about the questions about the data shown in the block graph. Then read 'Think like a scientist 2: How many legs?'. This asks learners to find some small animals and use a magnifying glass to count the legs before drawing their own block graph.

If necessary, re-read, with learners, the 'Science skills' section at the back of the Learner's Book. The part called 'How to draw a block graph' explains the process of drawing a block graph.

Safety: Make sure that learners are safe from hazards in any outdoor space they use. Make sure learners know how to behave safely around any animals or plants that could cause injury.

Take learners outside to find and observe small animals. Learners could use a tally chart like the one shown below to record their results.

0 legs	2 legs	4 legs	6 legs	8 legs
||			|||| ||	||

Ask learners to look at an animal with a classmate and check they agree on the number of legs they can see. If they disagree, ask them to look and count again, perhaps from a different angle, so they can see the legs more clearly.

Learners can use their tally charts to fill in a block graph similar to the one shown in the Learner's Book when they are back in the classroom. Draw a block graph on the board and show learners how to fill it in before asking them to do their own.

> **Practical guidance:** Show learners how to hold the magnifying glass close to the object they are looking at then move it closer or further away until they can see a clear focussed image.

If your school has no safe outdoor space where learners could find and observe small animals, prepare a worksheet with many photos of small animals taken from above against a white background. Ask learners to count the legs of these animals and make a block graph of this data instead.

> **Differentiation ideas:** You could support learners who find observation difficult by collecting some small animals in a clear container with a lid and looking at these carefully as a group. Alternatively, these learners could use enlarged photographs of small animals.

Some learners could be challenged to draw their own block graphs using squared paper.

> **Assessment ideas:** Assess learners' block graphs when you mark them by comparing them to their tally charts.

4   Workbook 4.1 (30 minutes)

Learning intention: We are going to use and make block graphs.

Resources: Workbook

Description: Learners can use the Focus and Practice activities in the workbook to practise drawing block graphs. The Challenge activity asks learners to read information from a block graph.

> **Assessment ideas:** You can use this activity to assess whether learners can use and make block graphs.

Plenary ideas

1   Reflection (10 minutes)

Resources: Learner's Book

Description: Read the Reflection section of the Learner's Book with learners. This explains that asking questions is an important part of science. Explain that science is about finding out about the world and that this always starts with a question about what we want to find out. Scientists try to make the world better by asking important questions such as 'How can we cure this illness?' or 'Do humans need trees to survive?'.

Ask learners 'Do you have any important science questions?'. Then talk about any questions they have.

2 Your favourite animal (10 minutes)

Description: Choose a learner to talk about their favourite animal. Ask 'What do you like about how it looks?'. Then choose another learner to talk about their favourite animal and how it looks different or similar to the first animal. You could sit the learners in one large or several small circles and ask them to go around their circle to talk about how their favourite animal is similar or different to the previous animal.

⟩ **Assessment ideas:** Assess learners by listening to their description of how their animal is similar or different to another.

CROSS-CURRICULAR LINKS

This topic could be linked with art work on pattern. Ask learners to observe and draw examples of the patterns found in the fur of different animals. You could use the zebra and giraffe fur shown in the Learner's Book as a starting point. Ask learners to talk about how the patterns are similar or different.

Homework ideas

Ask learners to draw two animals of their choice at home and label them to show how they are similar and how they are different.

Ask learners to record some data in a tally chart about different animals seen outside school. They could then fill in a block graph template showing the number of each animal they saw.

Topic worksheets

Worksheets 4.1A, 4.1B and 4.1C

These worksheets ask learners to identify similarities and differences in different animals.

Worksheet 4.1A asks learners to tick the correct sentence and put a cross next the incorrect sentence.

Worksheet 4.1B asks learners to write 'similar' or 'different' under the appropriate phrase for each pair of animals.

Worksheet 4.1C asks learners to write sentences identifying how the animals are similar and different.

4.2 Growing

LEARNING PLAN

Learning objectives	Learning intention	Success criteria
2Bp.03 Describe how the offspring of animals, including humans, change as they become older.	• We are going to learn how humans and other animals change as they grow.	• I can describe how humans and some animals change as they grow.
2TWSc.03 Take measurements in non-standard units.	• We are going to measure how tall we are using bottles.	• I can measure how tall a person is using bottles.
2TWSa.03 Present and interpret results using tables and block graphs.	• We are going to draw block graphs.	• I can draw a block graph.
2TWSa.02 Identify simple patterns in results, for example, increasing and decreasing patterns.	• We are going to find patterns in results.	• I can find patterns in results.

LANGUAGE SUPPORT

In this topic the word *young* is used both as an adjective and a noun. Learners may find this confusing, so explain early on in this topic that the adjective is the opposite of old and the noun means the babies of an animal. Keep the two definitions on display in the classroom. It may be helpful to remind learners of other words that they may know that can also be both nouns and adjectives, for example, orange, total and square.

adult: an animal that is fully grown and could become a parent

age: how many years a living thing has been alive

baby: a very young animal

calf: a young elephant, cow or whale is called a calf

chick: young birds are called chicks

cub: a young bear, wolf, lion or tiger is called a cub

grow/growth: changes that happen as living things get older

old/older: an animal that has been alive for a long time

parent: an animal's mother or father

pictogram: a way of showing results that uses pictures instead of numbers

young (adj): an animal that has not been alive for long

young (noun): an animal's babies are called its young

Common misconceptions

Misconception	How to identify	How to overcome
Some learners may think that older people are always taller than younger people.	Read the Learner's Book section about the human life cycle and drawing a block graph. Ask learners to estimate the height (in bottles) of an adult older than 30.	Explain that children grow taller but that human are fully grown at around 17–20 years old. After that they do not grow taller and may even get a little smaller as they go into old age. Show learners the picture showing changes in humans as they grow and point out that the oldest humans in the picture are not the tallest.

Starter ideas

1   Getting started (15 minutes)

Resources: Learner's Book

Description: Read the 'Getting started' section in the Learner's Book with learners. This shows a picture of a zoo with adult and baby animals. Ask learners to say how many baby animals they can see, then explain that a baby bear is called a cub and ask 'Can you name any other baby animals?'.

Next talk about how the babies are similar or different from the adults. Ask 'Which baby animals look like the adults? Which babies look different from the adults?'. Ask learners to talk in pairs about the answers, then choose learners to give feedback to the class.

2   Baby animals video (10 minutes)

Resources: Video of baby animals (search the internet for 'Baby animals in the wild video')

Description: Show learners a video of wild baby mammals or birds. Ask learners to talk about how the animals look and behave differently from the adults. Ask 'Will the baby animals stay the same or will they change?'. Ask learners to describe how the animals might change as they grow.

Main teaching ideas

1 Activity 1: How do baby animals change? (30 minutes)

Learning intention: We are going to learn how humans and other animals change as they grow.

Resources: Learner's Book, pictures of baby and adult animals, prepared worksheets with pictures of baby animals with their adults or Workbook: Topic 4.2, Digital Classroom activity: Adults and babies (optional)

Description: Read Activity 1 with learners. This shows how they can add notes to a picture of a baby and adult animal to show how the baby changes as it grow. Show learners the pictures of baby and adult animals and ask learners to suggest some changes that happen as animals grow. List some of their suggestions that are common to many animals on the board, for example, grows bigger, more fur, changes colour, finds own food.

Ask learners to use the prepared worksheets to make notes on how animals change as they grow. They could also use Workbook 4.2 Focus and Practice to develop their ideas about how animals change as they grow.

> **Digital Classroom:** If you have access to the Digital Classroom component, use the activity 'Adults and babies' with learners. Learners can use this activity to match baby animals with their adults. The i button will explain how to use the activity.

> **Assessment ideas:** During the activity, assess whether learners can describe how an animal changes as it grows. This can also be assessed when you mark their work.

2 Activity 2: A younger you (30 minutes)

Learning intention: We are going to learn how humans and other animals change as they grow.

Resources: Learner's Book, pictures of learners when they were younger, prepared worksheet for each learner with a copy of their younger picture and of a photo showing them as they are now (optional)

Description: Read Activity 2 with learners and talk about how the baby shown will change as it grows. Show learners some of the pictures of learners when

they were younger. Ask 'Who can tell me one way this learner is different now to their picture?'. Do this for several learners, before asking learners to work in pairs or small groups to talk about how they have changed as they have grown up.

If available, you could ask learners to label the copies of the pictures of themselves to show how they have changed.

> **Differentiation ideas:** If you think some learners will find it hard to identify how they have changed, use these learners as examples at the start of the activity. Ask other learners to identify how these learners have changed. If necessary, make notes for these learners to use in the discussion or in the labelling activity later.

Challenge learners who find it easy to identify changes to notice smaller changes such as face or nose shape.

> **Assessment ideas:** During the activity, talk with learners to assess whether they can describe how a human changes as it grows. This can also be assessed when you mark their work.

3 Think like a scientist: Measuring height (60 minutes)

Learning intention: We are going to measure how tall we are using bottles.

We are going to draw block graphs.

We are going to find patterns in results.

Resources: Some younger children, some adults and some 500 ml plastic bottles, block graph template, Workbook 4.2 Challenge (optional), Worksheet 4.2A, 4.2B or 4.2C (optional)

Description: Read the section in the Learner's Book about human growth and 'Think like a scientist: Measuring height' with learners. This shows how plastic bottles can be used as non-standard measure to measure people's height.

Speak to another teacher to arrange for some learners to measure the height of some younger children in the school. Arrange for some other learners to measure the height of some adults. Other learners could measure the height of some of their classmates. Record these measurements in a table on the board, for example,

Person	Younger learner	Stage 2 learner	Adult
Height	4 bottles	5 bottles	7 bottles

Ask learners to use the Block graph template to draw a block graph of these results. If necessary, re-read, with learners, the 'Science skills' section at the back of the Learner's Book. The part called 'How to draw a block graph' uses step by step instructions to show learners the process of drawing a block graph.

When learners have drawn their graphs, show an example and ask 'Can you see a pattern in the numbers?'. Explain, if necessary, that the height is going up as the age goes up and ask learners to finish this sentence describing the pattern: 'The older the person ... (the taller they grow)'. Explain that this pattern can be seen in the results and ask 'Is this pattern always true for all people or is it only true for some people?'. Choose eight learners and put them in a line in age order. Make it clear to learners that the oldest is at one end and the youngest at the other end then ask 'Are the older children taller?'. If the pattern is true in this sample of learners, add more learners to the line in the correct position according to their age until the pattern is interrupted. Explain to learners that, while most children grow taller as they get older, this does not mean that older people are *always* taller. Show the example block graph again and explain 'The pattern is true for these three people but it is not always true'.

Ask learners whether they know their grandparents. Say 'If this pattern was always true, then your grandparents would be taller than your parents. Are they?'. Explain that children grow taller until they become adults. As adults grow into old age, they stop getting taller and many become a little smaller.

Learners could now use Worksheets 4.2A, 4.2B or 4.2C to draw block graphs of different data. Choose which to use to suit each learner's ability.

Learners could use the Challenge activity in Workbook: Topic 4.2. This asks them to use the data shown in a block graph about the growth of a cat to answers questions.

> **Practical guidance:** Learners will find it easier to measure the height of a person if the person lies on the floor with their feet against the wall. They can then use only two bottles to 'mark out' how t all the person is. This process is shown in the Learner's Book.

Learners will find that some people are a little taller or a little shorter than a whole number of bottles. Demonstrate this for learners and explain how to 'round up' or 'round down' the measurement.

> **Differentiation ideas:** Support learners who find measuring difficult by getting them to make a whole line of bottles next to the person and then counting the number of bottles in the line.

Some learners could be challenged to measure people's height in centimetres and use the data to draw bar charts instead of block graphs.

> **Assessment ideas:** During the activity, ask learners to peer assess by checking each other's measurements with the bottles.

Observe learners to make sure they are measuring correctly. You can assess the block graphs when you mark learners' work.

Plenary ideas

1 Draw an older you (15 minutes)

Resources: pencils and paper

Description: Ask learners to think about how they might change as they grow older. You could perhaps show a photo of yourself as a child and ask them to say how you have changed now you are an adult.

Ask learners to draw a picture of an older version of themselves. They could choose to show what they might look like, whether they might have children themselves and/or what job they might do.

> **Assessment ideas:** Talk with learners to assess whether they can describe how children change as they grow into adults.

2 How are babies different from us? (10 minutes)

Resources: Video of babies laughing (search the internet for 'babies laughing video')

Description: Show learners a video of babies laughing. Then ask learners to describe how they have changed since they were babies. Ask 'What can you do now that you could not do as a baby?'.

> **Assessment ideas:** Talk with learners to assess whether they can describe how babies change as they grow into children.

CROSS-CURRICULAR LINKS

This topic has strong links with measuring in non-standard units in maths. 'Think like a scientist: Measuring height' is a great opportunity for learners to practise this essential maths skill.

Homework ideas

Ask learners to find a picture of themselves as a baby or as a younger child and bring it in to school to be used in Activity 2.

Ask learners to compare themselves to an older or younger member of their family and note how they are similar and how they are different. They could make notes by labelling drawings or photographs.

Topic worksheets

Worksheets 4.2A, 4.2B and 4.2C

Worksheet 4.2A asks learners to measure the height of the people and draw a corresponding block chart.

Worksheet 4.2B asks learners to do the same exercise but they must cut out the bottles and use them to measure the people.

Worksheet 4.2C asks learners to cut out a ruler and use this to measure the people.

4.3 Inheriting characteristics

LEARNING PLAN

Learning objectives	Learning intention	Success criteria
2Bp.04 Know that animals, including humans, produce offspring that have a combination of features from their parents.	• We are going to find out why animals look similar to their parents.	• I can explain why animals look similar to their parents.
2TWSc.01 Sort and group objects, materials and living things based on observations of the similarities and differences between them.	• We are going to put children into groups using characteristics.	• I can put children into groups using characteristics.

LANGUAGE SUPPORT

This topic introduces the word *fingerprint*. Explain to learners that this is an example of a compound word that is made from two others *finger+print*.

With learners, make a list of other familiar compound words. This might include the following examples *cannot, sometimes, anybody, football, sunflower, grandmother*.

CONTINUED

fingerprint: the pattern of lines in the skin of your fingers

identical: exactly the same

inherit: getting a characteristic from a parent when you are born

stripes: a pattern of lines

twins: two people with the same mother who were born at the same time

Note: Be sensitive to any learners who are looked after by carers, step-parents or their extended family rather than their parents. These learners may have photographs of their parents at home that they could use to compare how they look, or they could be asked to compare themselves with their grandparents or other relatives if appropriate.

Common misconceptions

Misconception	How to identify	How to overcome
Some learners may think that boys inherit characteristics only from their fathers and girls only from their mothers.	Ask learners to say how they are similar to their mother and to their father. Learners may say that they are only similar to one parent.	If possible, use photographs to point out ways that the learner is similar to both parents. If this is not possible, demonstrate this using other learners or using photographs of famous people. For example, say 'This learner's eyes and nose look like his father but his hair is curly like his mother'.
Many learners will think that if a baby animal has one parent with brown hair and one with black hair then the baby will have dark brown hair.	Talk with learners about why they think animals look different. Ask 'If a baby animal has dark brown hair, what colour hair might the parents have?'.	Explain that how we inherit characteristic from our parents is not simple. Usually a baby of one parent with brown hair and one with black hair will have either brown or black hair. Similarly a child of a tall woman and a short man is more likely to be either tall or short than to be of medium height.

Starter ideas

1 Getting started (10 minutes)

Resources: Learner's Book

Description: Read the 'Getting started' section of the Learner's Book with learners which shows a picture of some different sheep. Ask 'Why do you think the sheep look different?' or 'What would make a sheep have brown or black or white wool?'. Talk with learners to find out what they understand about inherited characteristics.

Look out for learners who think that a sheep's wool colour will be a mix of the parent's wool colour.

Explain that it is more likely that the sheep will have a similar wool colour to one parent or the other.

2 How are you like your parents? (10 minutes)

Description: Ask learners 'Do you look more like your Mum or your Dad? Can you say why?'.

Note: Be sensitive to learners who are looked after by people who are not their birth parents. These learners could compare themselves to other relatives or they might have photographs of their parents they can use to make comparisons.

Choose some learners to give examples then ask the class to answer the following questions.

- Do you have the same colour hair as your Dad?
- Do you have the same colour hair as your Mum?
- Does your nose look like your Mum or Dad's nose?
- Do your eyes look like your Mum or Dad's eyes?

Some learners may think that boys inherit characteristics only from their fathers and girls only from their mothers. If possible, use photographs to point out ways that the learner is similar to both parents. If this is not possible, demonstrate this using other learners or using photographs of famous people. For example say 'This learner's eyes and nose look like his father but his hair is curly like his mother'.

Main teaching ideas

1 Activity: How are you different? (60 minutes)

Learning intention: We are going to put children into groups using characteristics.

Resources: Learner's Book, mirrors, prepared table of results for learners to complete, Digital Classroom video: Similar characteristics (optional)

Description: Read in the Learner's Book about how our characteristics are inherited from our parents. Explain that because we inherit different characteristics from our parents, we all (except for identical twins) look different from other people, even from our brothers and sisters.

Read the activity in the Learner's Book then give learners mirrors so they can identify which characteristics they have of the five pictured: freckles, free/fixed earlobes, left/right handed, straight/curly hair, able to roll their tongue. Ask learners to complete the prepared table of results by writing yes or no for each question given in the Learner's Book.

1. Do you have freckles?
2. Are your earlobes free?
3. Are you left-handed?
4. Can you roll your tongue?
5. Do you have straight hair?

Demonstrate to learners how they can use these characteristics to make groups. Choose one

characteristic, for example, left or right handed, and ask all left handed learners to stand in one group and right handed learners to stand in another group.

Put learners into working groups of six to ten learners. Choose a different characteristic for each working group and ask them to sort themselves into two smaller groups based on the chosen characteristic. Review each working group's sorting with the class and ask other learners to check to make sure they have sorted themselves into the correct group.

Finish the activity by asking learners to write their own identity (ID) code based on their answers to the five questions given in the Learner's Book. They should use a letter N for an answer 'no' and a letter Y for an answer 'yes'. If their five answers were no, yes, no, no, yes then their ID code would be NYNNY. Make sure learners put their answers in the same order as the questions.

Ask learners to compare their ID codes to see whether any other learner has the same code as themselves. There are 32 different possible codes. This shows that people are different from each other. If some learners do have the same ID code, stand them next to each other and ask 'Do these learners look identical?'. Ask learners to identify ways that they look different.

> **Digital Classroom:** If you have access to the Digital Classroom component, use the video 'Similar characteristics' with learners. The photos show children from a range of different ethnic backgrounds with similar characteristics to their parents. The i button will explain how to use the video.

> **Differentiation ideas:** Learners who find it difficult to cooperate in large groups could work in smaller groups of four.

Some groups of learners could be challenged to sort themselves into four subgroups using two characteristics at once to create a Carroll Diagram. For example,

	I have straight hair	I have curly hair
I can roll my tongue		
I cannot roll my tongue		

> **Assessment ideas:** During the activity, assess learners by asking individuals to explain why a learner has been sorted into a specific group.

2 Think like a scientist: Sorting fingerprints (45 minutes)

Learning intention: We are going to put children into groups using our characteristics.

Resources: Learner's Book, balloons and marker pens, felt tip pens or ink pads, three areas of the classroom labelled with one of the three types of fingerprints: loop, whorl, arch, balloon pump (optional)

Description: Read 'Think like a scientist: Sorting fingerprints' in the Learner's Book with learners. This shows how a fingerprint on an uninflated balloon can be made larger by blowing up the balloon. Demonstrate this for learners and show the three main types of fingerprints: loop, whorl and arch. Ask learners to say which one the fingerprint shown in the photograph in the Learner's Book is most like.

Learners can now put their own fingerprint on a balloon and leave it a few seconds to dry. You can then inflate and tie the balloon for them. Learners can then write their name on their balloon, then make a drawing of their enlarged fingerprint on paper before sorting their fingerprint into the correct group. They could do this by putting their balloon in the part of the classroom labelled with their type of fingerprint.

> **Practical guidance:** Test the ink from different pens or ink pads before this activity to make sure it leaves a clear print. Ask learners to practise making fingerprints on paper before using the balloon. Learners should only use one finger to avoid getting lots of ink on their hands. Make sure they do not touch the fingerprints on the balloons while the ink is still wet.

Some learners will need help to inflate and tie their balloons. A balloon pump could be used.

> **Differentiation ideas:** Some learners may need support to follow the instructions on making a fingerprint correctly. These learners could be paired with others or could work in a group with an adult.

Challenge more observant learners to research and identify fingerprint sub-categories such as plain

arch, tented arch, ulnar loop, double loop and radial loop.

> **Assessment ideas:** After the activity, check each group of fingerprints with learners to make sure everyone has sorted their fingerprint into the correct group.

3 Workbook 4.3 (20 minutes)

Learning intention: We are going to find out why animals look similar to their parents.

We are going to put children into groups using characteristics.

Resources: Workbook

Description: Learners can use the Focus activity to practise the vocabulary from this topic. The Practice section asks learners to identify which parent children inherited characteristics from. In the Challenge section learners will use fingerprints to sort learners into groups.

> **Assessment ideas:** You can assess learners' progress by marking their work.

Plenary ideas

1 Reflection (5 minutes)

Resources: Learner's Book

Description: Read the reflection section of the Learner's Book with learners. This reminds learners that balloons were used in Think like a scientist 1 to make fingerprints larger. It asks them to suggest a different way to make a fingerprint look larger. Learners should be able to suggest using a magnifying glass as they should have experience of using these.

Ask learners 'Why is it useful to make things larger to see them?'. Explain, if necessary, that when things are larger, we are more likely to notice small details in what we are looking at.

2 'Crime' scene (10 minutes)

Resources: Balloons with fingerprints of each learner from 'Think like a scientist: Sorting fingerprints', an enlarged fingerprint of one learner

Description: Before this activity choose a learner to be the 'mystery person'. Do not let other learners know who the 'mystery person' is. Take a fingerprint from this learner on paper, then photograph or enlarge it on a photocopier and display it on the board. Tell learners 'Something has happened in the classroom and I need to find out who did it.'. Explain that you have a fingerprint, but you need help to work out who's fingerprint it is. Show the enlarged fingerprint and ask learners to compare it to the enlarged named fingerprints on the balloons from 'Think like a scientist: Sorting fingerprints'. Ask learners to say who they think the 'mystery person' is.

When learners guess the 'mystery person' ask the 'mystery person' to stand up and then reveal that what happened was that they left an apple for you on your desk and that you want to say 'Thank you'.

CROSS-CURRICULAR LINKS

This topic has links with social and moral education work on equality and acceptance of others. You could use this topic as a starting point for further work about the importance of tolerance and diversity. Further activities could include finding out about different languages spoken by learners in school, exploring stereotypes with learners by asking them to suggest whether certain jobs are seen as a man's job or a woman's job and asking them how these stereotypes might be challenged, and reading stories that challenge perceptions such as the traditional tale of the Hare and the Tortoise.

Homework ideas

Ask learners to draw a picture of themselves and a parent or a grandparent. Ask them to include labels that show characteristics they have inherited from that parent.

Ask learners to find out whether their parents or other family members have the five characteristics from the 'How are you different?' activity. Learners could use the same worksheet they used themselves during the activity and work out a family member's ID code.

4.4 Keeping healthy

LEARNING PLAN

Learning objectives	Learning intention	Success criteria
2Bp.01 Know that humans need to manage diet, maintain hygiene and move regularly to be healthy.	• We are going to find out how to keep healthy.	• I can talk about three ways to keep healthy.
2Bp.02 Describe what illness is and describe the common signs of illness in humans.	• We are going to find out why humans get ill and what it does to our bodies.	• I can say why humans get ill and what being ill does to our bodies.

CONTINUED

Learning objectives	Learning intention	Success criteria
2TWSc.01 Sort and group objects, materials and living things based on observations of the similarities and differences between them.	• We are going to sort food into groups.	• I can sort food into groups.
2TWSa.01 Describe what happened during an enquiry and if it matched their predictions.	• We are going to say if our predictions are correct or not.	• I can say if my predictions are correct or not.

LANGUAGE SUPPORT

In English there are several different phrases that can be used when someone is ill. 'I feel poorly' and 'I don't feel very well' are both commonly used. The phrase 'I feel sick,' is often used to mean 'I feel ill,' rather than describing the feeling of sickness specifically. Talk with learners to find out which of these phrases they are familiar with, if any. Use any familiar phrases throughout the topic when talking about illness.

clean: not dirty

diet: the food we eat

exercise: moving around using your muscles

germs: very small living things that can make you ill

headache: when your head hurts

heart: part of our bodies that pumps blood around our body to help keep us alive

ill/illness: not feeling well, not being well

muscles: part of our bodies that can make us move

sick: being sick is when your body pushes everything in your tummy out through your mouth

sweat: when your skin become wet because you are hot or ill

Common misconceptions

Misconception	How to identify	How to overcome
Many learners will think that people should never eat food that is thought of as unhealthy. In fact, humans need a varied diet, but most people eat too much unhealthy food.	Talk with learners about food that is healthy or unhealthy for humans. Ask them to talk about how much of each type of food they think a person should eat.	Use the food triangle in the Learner's Book to explain about the need for a varied diet that includes a balance of food from different food groups.

Starter ideas

1 Getting started (10 minutes)

Resources: Learner's Book

Description: Show learners the 'Getting started' picture in the Learner's Book that shows children saying what they think about healthy food. Read the speech bubbles with learners and ask them to say whether they agree or disagree with each of the statements, or whether they have different ideas.

Ask 'Is it ok to eat chocolate/cake/sweets ever?'. Discuss children's ideas about these unhealthy foods.

Many learners will think that people should never eat food that is thought of as unhealthy. In fact, humans need a varied diet, but most people eat too much unhealthy food. Use the food triangle in the Learner's Book to explain about the need for a varied diet that includes a balance of food from different food groups.

2 Being ill (10 minutes)

Resources: Learner's Book

Description: Ask learners 'Have you ever been ill/poorly/unwell?'. Ask learners to talk about what their illness did to their bodies, for example, sickness, feeling hot or cold, sweaty, headache tummy ache, etc.

Find out what learners know about the causes of illnesses by asking 'Why do you think people get ill? What makes that happen?'.

Main teaching ideas

1 Activity: Sorting food (30 minutes)

Learning intention: We are going to find out how to keep healthy.

We are going to sort food into groups.

Resources: Learner's Book, each group of learners will need cards labelled 'Eat lots', 'Eat some' and 'Eat a little' and pictures or samples of different food for example, different fruit and vegetables, some pasta, noodles, rice and bread, some meat, fish, chicken, dried beans, milk and eggs and some oil, butter, cake and sweets, Digital Classroom – Healthy food (optional)

Description: Read the 'Activity: Sorting food' in the Learner's Book with learners. This shows how to sort food into three groups: food we should eat a lot of, food we should eat some of and food of which we should eat only a little.

Put learners into pairs or small groups and ask them to sort their food pictures or samples into these three different groups. Remind them to use the food triangle in the Learner's Book to help them.

After a few minutes, ask if there are any foods that learners are not sure about and share learner's ideas about which group these should go into with the class. Explain the correct answer if necessary.

Learners could record their work by sticking pictures of food into the three groups or

drawing labelled pictures of their sorted food samples.

> **Digital Classroom:** If you have access to the Digital Classroom component, use the activity 'Healthy food' with learners. Learners can use this activity to identify foods that are healthy. The i button will explain how to use the activity.

> **Differentiation ideas:** You could pair learners who need more support with more confident learners in this activity or they could work in a larger group guided by you or another adult.

Some learners could be challenged to sort the foods into the four food groups shown in the food triangle: fats and sugar, protein, carbohydrates, vitamins and minerals.

> **Assessment ideas:** While learners are working, observe how they are sorting the food to assess whether they are sorting correctly.

2 Being ill (30 minutes)

Learning intention: We are going to find out why humans get ill and what it does to our bodies.

Resources: Learner's Book, Worksheets 4.4A, 4.4B and 4.4C (optional)

Description: Read with learners the 'Being ill' section in the Learner's Book. This explains about the common signs of illness, and how germs can make us ill. Talk with learners about different ways we try to stop germs getting into our bodies: washing hands after going to the toilet and before eating, cleaning cuts and grazes and covering our mouths when we sneeze or cough.

Ask learners to draw a picture of an ill person and label it with the common signs of illness. Learners could use Worksheet 4.4B. This asks them to match labels of the common signs of illness to pictures.

> **Differentiation ideas:** Learners who need more support could use Worksheet 4.4A. This supports them by giving the first letter of each label.

Some learners could be challenged to use Worksheet 4.4C, where they have to identify the signs of illness independently.

> **Assessment ideas:** You can assess whether learners can identify the common signs of illness when you mark their work.

3 Think like a scientist: What happens when we exercise? (40 minutes)

Learning intention: We are going to find out how to keep healthy.

We are going to say if our predictions are correct or not.

Resources: Learner's Book, a timer, watch or clock, a large indoor or outdoor space, a picture of a child exercising for each learner to label, heart rate monitor (optional), Digital Classroom animation – 'Keeping healthy' (optional)

Description: Read 'Think like a scientist: What happens when we exercise?' in the Learner's Book with learners. This explains that learners should look out for changes in their breathing, their heart beat and their skin when they exercise. Ask learners to make predictions about how these things might change and talk to a partner about their predictions.

Take learners to a large space and explain that they are going to exercise for three minutes. As soon as they stop say 'Feel your heart. How fast is it beating now? How does your skin feel now? Is your breathing fast or slow?'. Choose learners to share their answers with the class, then ask learners to talk with their partner about the predictions they made earlier and whether these are correct. Explain that if their predictions were not correct, this could show that they have learnt something new.

Learners could record what happens when we exercise by labelling a picture of a child exercising to show the changes that happen.

⟩ **Digital Classroom:** If you have access to the Digital Classroom component, use the animation 'Keeping healthy' with learners. The animation demonstrates the effects of exercise on the body. Stop the animation at the 'Pause for thought' sections so learners can answer the questions. The i button will explain how to use the animation.

⟩ **Practical guidance:** In this activity, you could direct learners in a series of different exercises that do not involve moving around such as running on the spot, star jumps, straight jumps, etc. Alternatively, learners could choose their own exercise for three minutes. Use a timer and tell learners when to start and when to stop.

Show learners how to feel their heart beat by placing a hand in the centre of their chest.

⟩ **Differentiation ideas:** You could support learners who have difficulty feeling their heart beat by showing them how to feel their pulse, by using a heart rate monitor or by using a heart rate monitor app on a tablet computer.

You could challenge some learners to measure their heart rate by counting how many times they feel it beat in a minute.

⟩ **Assessment ideas:** Assess learners by asking them to say what changes they notice when they exercise and by marking their labelled pictures of a child exercising.

4 Workbook 4.4 (45 minutes)

Learning intention: We are going to find out how to keep healthy.

We are going to find out why humans get ill and what it does to our bodies.

We are going to sort food into groups.

Resources: Workbook

Description: Learners can use the Focus activity to sort food into groups. The Practice section asks them to plan their own healthy meal. The Challenge section is a crossword that learners can use to show their understanding of some of the key words in this topic.

⟩ **Assessment ideas:** While learners are working, assess whether learners understand how to be healthy by asking them individually to tell you three different ways they can keep healthy.

Plenary ideas

1 Can we be more healthy? (10 minutes)

Resources: Learner's Book

Description: Ask, 'How could you make your diet more healthy? Do you keep your body clean? Do you do some exercise every day?' then ask, 'What could you do to be more healthy?'. Some learners may be reluctant to share their response with the class, so explain that you are not going to ask them to say what they think they should do more often unless they want to.

2 Why do we like unhealthy food? (10 minutes)

Description: Ask learners to tell a partner about their favourite food. Then choose some learners to share their favourite food with the class. When a learner chooses an unhealthy food, for example, chocolate, French fries, ice cream or sweets ask, 'Who else likes this?'. Then name some other unhealthy foods and ask learners to show whether they like them. Explain that most people like the taste of food with lots of fat and sugar, but eating lots of them would be unhealthy for our bodies.

Finish by asking learners to name their favourite healthy food and remind them that they can eat lots of these types of food.

> Assessment ideas: Look out for learners who fail to name a healthy food when asked to do so.

CROSS-CURRICULAR LINKS

The exercise section of this topic has links with physical exercise (P.E.). You could use this topic to start a regular five to ten-minute exercise routine with your class. This could be done daily or several times a week.

Homework ideas

Ask learners to keep a food diary recording the types of food they eat over a week.

Ask learners to keep an exercise diary recording the type of exercise they do each day and for how long. Alternatively, they could draw a picture of their favourite type of exercise and label it with the effect it has on their body.

Topic worksheets

Worksheets 4.4A, 4.4B and 4.4C

The majority of learners should be able to complete Worksheet 4.4B, which asks them to match labels of the common signs of illness to pictures.

Learners who need more support could use Worksheet 4.4A. This supports them by giving the first letter of each label.

Some learners could be challenged to use Worksheet 4.4C, where they have to identify the signs of illness indicated on the images and write sentences about the symtoms.

4.5 Teeth

LEARNING PLAN

Learning objectives	Learning intention	Success criteria
2Bs.02 Identify the different types of human teeth, explain how they are suited to their functions and describe how to care for teeth.	• We are going to learn about the different types of teeth and what they do. • We are going to learn about how to look after teeth.	• I can describe the three types of teeth and what the different types do. • I can explain how to look after my teeth.
2TWSa.01 Describe what happened during an enquiry and if it matched their predictions.	• We are going to say if our predictions are correct or not.	• I can say if my predictions are correct or not.
2TWSm.02 Make and use a physical model of a familiar system or idea. **2TWSm.01** Know that a model represents an object or idea in a clear way.	• We are going to observe human teeth and make models of them.	• I can make model teeth and say how the model teeth are like real teeth.

LEARNING PLAN

Learning objectives	Learning intention	Success criteria
2TWSc.04 Follow instructions safely when doing practical work.	• We are going to investigate teeth safely.	• I can stay safe when I do an investigation.

LANGUAGE SUPPORT

This topic provides an opportunity for learners to write commands/instructions such as 'Brush your teeth twice a day' or 'Go to the dentist'. Explain to learners that this type of sentence always starts with the verb and has no subject (you, I, he or she, etc.). This is called the imperative form of the verb. Teachers sometime call it the 'Bossy verb' because it tells people what to do in a way that can sound impolite.

calcium: something found in milk and other dairy food that helps teeth grow strong

canine: a type of tooth with a pointed top for gripping food

dairy: food that has milk in it or food that is made from milk

dentist: a doctor who looks after people's teeth

fluoride: something found in some toothpastes which makes teeth stronger

gums: the part of the mouth that teeth grow from

incisor: a type of tooth with a flat sharp top for biting food

molar: a type of tooth with a wide lumpy top for chewing food

toothpaste: something to put on a toothbrush to help clean teeth and make them strong

Common misconceptions

Misconception	How to identify	How to overcome
Some learners will think that it doesn't matter if their baby teeth become damaged by too much sugar because another set of teeth will grow.	In the 'Getting started' activity or 'Think like a scientist 1', ask learners 'Does it matter if your teeth are damaged by sugar?'.	Explain to learners that, before adult teeth can be seen, they are growing in the gums. They can be damaged by sugar before they appear.

Starter ideas

1 Getting started (15 minutes)

Resources: Learner's Book, paper and pencils, class whiteboard/blackboard

Description: Read the 'Getting started' section of the Learner's Book with learners and ask learners to look at the picture. Ask 'What do you know about teeth?'. Choose two or three learners to share their ideas. If they say something that is not correct, say 'That's interesting. Does anyone agree with what (learner's name) said?'. Do not correct the misconception at this stage, but make a note to return to it in a later activity.

Find out what learners already know about teeth, including any misconceptions by asking them to draw a diagram of human teeth and label it with what they know about teeth.

At the end of the activity write three titles on the board 'Looking after teeth', 'Types of teeth' and 'Changes as you grow'. Ask learners to share some of their facts with the class and discuss whether other learners agree or disagree. Write correct facts on the board under the relevant heading. Make it clear to learners that the facts on the board are all correct.

Some learners will think that it doesn't matter if their baby teeth become damaged by too much sugar because another set of teeth will grow.

2 Losing teeth (10 minutes)

Description: Ask learners 'Has anyone had a tooth fall out or seen that happen to an older brother or sister? Why do you think it happens?'. Find out what learners understand by listening to their answers and asking others whether they agree or disagree with the ideas. Tell learners that you will explain why children's teeth fall out later in this topic.

Some learners will think that it doesn't matter if their baby teeth become damaged by too much sugar because another set of teeth will grow.

Main teaching ideas

1 Looking after teeth (45 minutes)

Learning intention: We are going to learn about how to look after teeth.

Resources: Learner's Book, blank paper, Worksheet 4.5A, 4.5B, 4.5C (optional)

Description: Read the 'Looking after teeth' section of the Learner's Book with learners and talk about the answers to the questions. Ask learners to make a poster showing others all the different things they can do to look after their teeth. Learners could use Worksheet 4.5A, 4.5B or 4.5C.

⟩ **Differentiation ideas:** Learners who need more support could use Worksheet 4.5A, which allows them to cut and stick sentences with the correct picture. Learners who have better developed English skills could use Worksheet 4.5C, which gives less support and asks learners to write why it is important to look after teeth.

⟩ **Assessment ideas:** Assess whether learners understand how to look after their teeth by talking to individuals while they are making the posters and by marking their work.

2 Think like a scientist 1: What does sugar do to teeth?

Timing: 20 minutes to set up. 20 minutes to review the results after 7 days.

Learning intention: We are going to learn about how to look after teeth.

We are going to say if our predictions are correct or not.

Resources: Learner's Book, egg shells, a drink with lots of sugar for example, cola (not diet), water, some cups or glasses, spoons. Digital Classroom activity: Healthy for teeth or not? (optional)

Description: Read 'Think like a scientist 1: What does sugar do to teeth?' with learners. This explains how to do the investigation. Make it clear to learners that egg shells are made of the same material as teeth, so whatever happens to the egg shell will be similar to what would happen to a tooth.

Learners should place half an egg shell in one cup with water and the other half in a cup with a sugary drink. These are then left for a week to see what happens. Ask learners to draw a labelled diagram of both the shell in water and the shell in sugary drink to show their predictions.

After a week, learners can use spoons to remove the egg shells from the cups. They could draw and label them next to their predictions.

Ask learners to talk in pairs about whether their predictions were correct or not. Choose some learners to tell the class.

⟩ **Digital Classroom:** If you have access to the Digital Classroom component, use the activity 'Healthy for teeth or not? with learners. Learners can use this activity identify food and drink that is good or bad for their teeth. The i button will explain how to use the activity.

⟩ **Practical guidance:** This investigation could be done as a demonstration for the whole class, or learners could work in groups. Each group could investigate the effects of a different sugary drink on the egg shell. They could then compare their results with those of other groups at the end.

⟩ **Differentiation ideas:** Learners who need support could work in a teacher-led group.

Learners who are good at maths could be asked to plan a similar investigation comparing the amount of sugar, as shown on the label, with the effect the drink has on an egg shell.

⟩ **Assessment ideas:** Ask learners to show on their work which of their predictions were correct and which were not. They could do this by putting a tick next to correct predictions and a cross next to incorrect ones. You can then assess this when marking their work.

3 Think like a scientist 2: Making model teeth (45 minutes)

Learning intention: We are going to learn about the different types of teeth and what they do.

We are going to observe human teeth and make models of them.

We are going to investigate teeth safely.

Resources: Learner's Book, mirrors and modelling clay

Description: Read the types of teeth section of the Learner's Book with learners. This describes and explains the function of incisors, canines and molars. Explain to learners why baby teeth have no root when they fall out. This is because a developing adult tooth grows below a baby tooth in the gum, causing the root to die back. This makes the baby tooth become loose and eventually fall out.

Now read 'Think like a scientist 2: Making model teeth'. This demonstrates how learners can use modelling clay to make a set of teeth. Encourage learners to use mirrors to observe their own teeth carefully and, with clean hands, touch and feel their own teeth.

Safety: Learners should wash their hands before touching their teeth. Warn learners not to touch other learners' teeth.

When learners have made their models, show them how to put them on paper and then label the different types of teeth.

⟩ **Practical guidance:** Demonstrate how learners should make the model. Start by making a thick curved line of modelling clay for the gum and use a pencil to make ten root holes for the teeth. Then show how to roll one end of a small lump of clay to make a conical root before shaping the top of the tooth. The teeth can then be pushed into the root holes made in the gum.

⟩ **Differentiation ideas:** Learners who need help with making things could be asked to make a gum with root holes and could be supported by others who could

make a set of teeth for these learners to put in the correct places. These learners could make a set of teeth that are larger than real teeth, so the shaping is easier.

Some learners could be challenged to make labels for their models, showing the names and functions of the different types of teeth.

⟩ **Assessment ideas:** Assess whether learners can name and talk about the functions of the different types of teeth by talking to individuals while they are working.

4 Workbook 4.5 (20 minutes)

Learning intention: We are going to learn about the different types of teeth and what they do.

Resources: Workbook

Description: Learners can use Workbook 4.5. The Focus task asks learners to match teeth to their picture and function. Learners can use the Practice activity to show they understand key words from this topic. The Challenge activity asks learners to identify types of teeth in an X-ray.

⟩ **Assessment ideas:** You can assess learners' progress by marking their work.

Plenary ideas

1 Reflection (10 minutes)

Resources: Learner's Book

Description: Read the 'Reflection' in the Learner's Book with learners. Explain to learners that many scientists make and use models to help answer questions. For example, some doctors use 3D printed models of body parts to work out how to do an operation, climate scientists use computers to model how the climate might change.

Ask learners to say what they learned from making their set of model teeth. Then ask, 'How is the model similar to real teeth?' and 'How is the model different to real teeth?'. This last question should help learners understand that all models have limitations. For example, real teeth are hard and strong, but the model teeth are soft and weak. When using models, it is important to recognise the limitations of the model.

> Assessment ideas: To assess whether learners can say how the model teeth are like real teeth, you could ask them to work in pairs to discuss or make a list of similarities. You can then observe the discussions or review the lists they produce.

2 Animal teeth (10 minutes)

Resources: Pictures of animal teeth for example, elephants, sharks, sheep and tigers

Description: Show learners some pictures of animal teeth. Ask 'Why do some animals have different types of teeth?'. Remind learners, if necessary, that different shaped teeth do different jobs. For example, you could say 'Tigers have long sharp canine teeth to grip and hold onto to animals they catch to eat. Sheep have incisors to bite grass and molars to chew it but no canines because they do not eat other animals.'.

Explain that you can see whether an animal eats meat, eats plants or eats both by looking at their teeth.

> Assessment ideas: Ask learners to name the different types of human teeth and describe their functions.

CROSS-CURRICULAR LINKS

The amount of sugar in food or drinks can be linked to non-standard measures in maths. You could create a display to show how many teaspoons of sugar are in different drinks or foods. Labels often show the amount of sugar present in the food or drink item.

Homework ideas

Learners could keep a toothbrush diary, recording what time and for how long they brush their teeth and whether they use toothpaste.

If appropriate, you could ask learners to observe the teeth of an adult at home. They could draw a diagram of the teeth and label how they are different to baby teeth. Explain to learners that some adults may not be happy to show them their teeth, so they should ask politely and ask someone else if the adult says no.

Topic worksheets

Worksheets 4.5A, 4.5B and 4.5C

Learners who need more support could use Worksheet 4.5A, which allows them to cut and stick sentences with the correct picture on the poster.

Most learners should be able to complete Worksheet 4.5B, which asks them to label the pictures on the poster using given words.

Learners who have better developed English skills could use Worksheet 4.5C, which gives less support and asks learners to write why it is important to look after teeth.

PROJECT: PEOPLE WHO USE SCIENCE

2SIC.03 Know that everyone uses science and identify people who use science professionally.

Learners will need blank paper and books about different jobs or access to the internet.

Read the project in the Learner's Book with learners. This has photographs of people who use science in their job. Each job is related to the topics in this unit; a dentist, a sports coach, a forensic police officer and a zoologist. Talk with learners about other jobs they know about that use science such as a doctor, nurse, cook or engineer.

Ask learners to choose a job and use books or the internet to find out more about how it uses science. Learners can then make a poster with a picture and notes about how the job uses science.

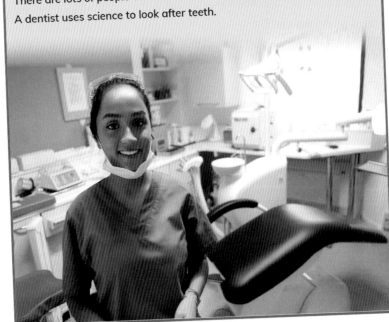

Project: People who use science

Look what I can do!

- [ ] I can describe the three types of teeth and what they do.
- [ ] I can explain how to look after my teeth.
- [ ] I can say if my predictions are correct or not.
- [ ] I can make model teeth and say how they are like real teeth.
- [ ] I can stay safe when I do an investigation.

Project: People who use science

There are lots of people who use science in their jobs.

A dentist uses science to look after teeth.

117 >

> 5 Light

Unit plan

Topic	Approximate number of learning hours	Outline of learning content	Resources
5.1 Light sources	2	Learners are introduced to a range of light sources and to a test of the brightness of flashlights.	**Learner's Book:** Activity 1: Is it a light source? Activity 2: So many light sources Think like a scientist: Which flashlight is brighter? **Workbook:** Topic 5.1 **Teacher's Resource:** ⬇ Worksheets 5.1A, 5.1B, 5.1C
5.2 Darkness	2	Learners look for dark areas in school and test the effect of darkness on our ability to see things.	**Learner's Book:** Activity 1: Darkness in our classroom Activity 2: Using a dark box Think like a scientist: How much light do I need to see? **Workbook:** Topic 5.2 **Teacher's Resource:** ⬇ Worksheets 5.2A, 5.2B, 5.2C **Digital Classroom:** Song – We can't see when the lights go out Animation – Can you see in the dark?
5.3 The Sun appears to move!	2	Learners observe the apparent movement of the Sun during the day.	**Learner's Book:** Activity: Looking at patterns Think like a scientist: Showing how the Sun appears to move! **Workbook:** Topic 5.3 **Teacher's Resource:** ⬇ Worksheets 5.3A, 5.3B, 5.3C

Across Unit resources
Learner's Book:
Project: My book of light
Check your progress quiz
Teacher's Resource:
⬓ Language worksheets 1 and 2
⬓ Diagnostic check
Digital Classroom:
⬓ End-of-unit quiz

BACKGROUND KNOWLEDGE

Light always travels from a light source. However, some bright objects like the Moon (which can give us light) are not light sources because they reflect light (for example, from the Sun). This unit refers to very bright light sources and to others which are not as bright. Whenever you can, warn learners never to look directly at very bright light sources such as the Sun because looking directly at such light sources can damage eyes.

Darkness occurs when there is little or no light. Many learners rarely experience complete darkness, because, even at night, we have starlight, moonlight and various electric lights. Learners may not realise that darkness is quite variable, from low light levels where reading a book is difficult, to complete darkness.

This topic follows on from Stage 1 Unit 1 which looked at light sources, including the Sun. You will need to know that the Sun is an important light source for us and for life on Earth. It is important for animals and for plants (which make their energy using sunlight). The Sun remains still relative to the Earth. Planet Earth spins anti-clockwise once each day and it takes one year to travel around (orbit) the Sun in an anti-clockwise direction.

In this topic, you may need to mention the apparent movement of the Sun in the sky. When you talk to the learners about the apparent movement of the Sun, try to refer to how the Sun appears to move, so that you avoid saying that is does move. Learners are asked to be aware of where the Sun is in the sky, without looking at it directly (it is safe to look into the sky and so be aware of the Sun's position, without looking directly at it). Another clue to the Sun's position is the direction of shadows we see on the ground. A shadow to the right of an object indicates that the Sun is to the left of the object.

You should know that the Sun remains still in relation to planet Earth. The Sun's apparent movement is caused by the Earth spinning. This explanation is taught in Stage 4. However, if learners ask you or claim that the Sun really does move, you should explain that the apparent movement is caused by the spinning of the Earth.

TEACHING SKILLS FOCUS

Active learning

Anticipate challenge

Like much of physical science, this topic can be a little abstract because learners cannot visit outer space. There is further complication because misconceptions are often held. For example, each day the Sun appears to move but it does not actually move. Use posters, models and role play as part of active learning. Ensure each lesson has active thinking as well as active doing. Encourage this thinking with open questions. For example, why do shadows start longer and get shorter during the morning?

Role play

In this unit there are opportunities for role play, that is, learners taking on the role of the Sun and the Earth. Ask learners to move as planets, but from time to time call out 'freeze frame' and ask the actors or spectators to explain what is happening at that point.

Language awareness

Some ideas here may be new or unfamiliar, so make time in lesson for learners to talk and ask questions. Use 'snowballing', that is, give learners time to talk in pairs or small groups and then to talk in larger groups, before coming back to class.

Metacognition

Give learners responsibility

If you use posters to summarise or convey ideas learners are learning, as well as role play, there will be many opportunities to talk about what learners already know, are thinking and are learning. Encourage learners to take responsibility for their own learning. For example, use a KWL chart (an example is given below) and ask learners to list:

- K (what they already know)
- W (what they want to learn) and
- after the lesson or series of lessons, L (what they have learned).

Keep this under review lesson by lesson or week by week. It will assist with assessment for learning, but also encourage learners to think about what they have learned.

Our science topic about ...		
K	W	L
What I already know	What I would like to know	What I have learnt

Get learners to think about how they learn science

The topic includes prompts to get learners to think about their learning. For example, how does a role play assist with my learning? Does it help me to see one thing move and how that affects other things? Does it help me raise useful questions?

Reflect on your teaching

During and after this unit, consider those elements of lessons to which learners responded well. Are these elements ones you can build into future science units?

5.1 Light sources

LEARNING PLAN

Learning objectives	Learning intention	Success criteria
2Pe.01 Identify how we use electricity and describe how to be safe with it.	• We are going to find light sources powered by electricity.	• I can find light sources powered by electricity.
2Ps.01 Know that there are many light sources, including the Sun.	• We are going to find different light sources, including the Sun.	• I can talk about different light sources, including the Sun.
2TWSc.06 Collect and record observations and/or measurements by annotating images and completing simple tables.	• We are going to record observations on a table.	• I can record observations on a table.
2TWSc.01 Sort and group objects, materials and living things based on observations of the similarities and differences between them.	• We are going to sort objects into groups.	• I can sort objects into groups.
2TWSc.02 Use given equipment appropriately.	• We are going to use given equipment to make observations.	• I can use equipment to make observations.
2TWSc.04 Follow instructions safely when doing practical work.	• We are going to follow instructions safely when doing practical work.	• I can follow instructions safely when doing practical work.

LANGUAGE SUPPORT

Make a labelled collection of light sources, perhaps including: flashlights, a picture of a lit candle, a picture of a lit match, a picture of the Sun, a tablet computer, a glow stick, etc. Label them and include sentences to reinforce meaning and show how they are used. For example, 'We use a flashlight at night'.

Make a collection of non-light sources, perhaps including: a fluorescent jacket, silver paper, a picture of the Moon, a silver cup, a metal spoon, etc. Include an explanation. For example, 'These shiny objects reflect light. They are not light sources'.

Make digital video recordings of learners talking about filmed light sources and non-light source for example, 'This is a mini flashlight, it is a light source'. Allow learners to play these back.

Use the language support worksheets as posters in class, as table-top vocabulary support, or as a bingo style game. For example, you could make sheets that contain six of the words from the language worksheets (different sheets should have different words on them). Cut out all the words from the language worksheet and put them in a container. Take out one word at a time and read it aloud to the learners. Learners who have that word on their sheet tick it.

CONTINUED

bright: a bright object gives off a lot of light, opposite to dull

flashlight: a device which makes light

light source: an object which makes light

Moon: large body which orbits Earth and which, on most nights, reflects light to Earth

reflect: light changing direction after hitting a surface

shine: making or reflecting light

Common misconceptions

Misconception	How to identify	How to overcome
Learners may confuse a light switch as a light source.	If you ask learners to identify light sources in a room, they may point to the light switch.	Ask the learners to observe where the light comes from and that this is not the switch but the electric light bulb.
Learners may consider that reflective materials or surfaces are light sources, for example, fluorescent jackets, the Moon.	When talking about reflective surfaces, for example, the Moon, many learners will say it is a light source.	Use a flashlight or other real light source to show how it shines on and illuminates a surface, for example, a ball of silver foil.

Starter ideas

1 How many light sources? (5–10 minutes)

Resources: Learner's Book, real examples including a flashlight, a mobile phone screen, a laptop screen, a lit candle, a lit match (optional)

Description: Ask learners to look at the illustration before Activity 1 that shows a night time street scene. Ask learners, in pairs, to examine the picture and to look for different light sources. Learners may identify any bright looking object as a light source, for example, a reflective number plate. Remind learners that a light source is something that makes light. Ask different pairs to feedback to the class with a light source. They should find the following: electric light bulb in a room, car headlights, a flashlight, a street light, a fire, rear light on a cycle, stars in the night sky. Note: planets (which are not light sources) can appear as bright lights in the night sky, for example, Venus. Learners should clearly see a range of light sources. Optional – you could show real examples including a flashlight, a mobile phone screen, a laptop screen, a lit candle, a lit match (warn learners never to play with flames).

2 These are not light sources (5–10 minutes)

Resources: Learner's Book, a reflective sign, a reflective jacket and flashlight (optional)

Description: Ask learners to look at the set of four pictures close to the start of this topic, which include the Moon and a reflective jacket. Say that these things are all bright and people may think they are light sources. They are not light sources, but can learners explain why they are bright? They should explain that this light is reflected from another source. For example, light from the Sun or another light source. If you have some real life examples, you can show, by shining a flashlight on them, that they reflect light well. You can point out that light colours and highly reflective materials are good to wear at night for road safety.

You may find some learners resistant to the idea that the Moon is not a light source because they are so familiar with it shining at night. Explain that the Moon is made of rock. There is no burning light source on the Moon.

Main teaching ideas

1 Activity 1: Is it a light source?
(10–15 minutes)

Learning intention: We are going to find different light sources, including the Sun.

We are going to find light sources powered by electricity.

We are going to sort objects into groups.

Resources: Learner's Book, examples of light sources, and objects that are not light sources, for example, a burning candle, mirror, computer, a spoon, a burning match, a reflective sign, a fluorescent jacket, any other shiny objects, two large plastic hoops (or large sheets of paper each with a large circle drawn on it), Workbook 5.1 Focus (optional), Worksheets 5.1A, 5.1B and 5.1C (optional)

Description: You could ask learners to complete Workbook 5.1 Focus, which asks learners to label light sources and then select one light source to draw.

Read the description of the activity in the Learner's Book.

Ask the learners to look at the different objects and materials and to discuss whether the objects and materials are light sources or not. Be very clear by saying 'this is a light source because it makes light'. Invite learners to use similar phrases for example, 'the candle burns which makes light, it is a source of light'. At this point you could use the Workbook 5.1 Practice activity, which asks learners to identify light sources, and not light sources.

You could ask learners to complete Worksheet 5.1A, which asks learners to identify things as light sources or not light sources, Worksheet 5.1B which asks learners to say why some things are light sources and others not, or Worksheet 5.1C, which asks learners to group things as not light sources, light sources which are bright, and light sources which are not bright.

Make two groups for objects using plastic hoops or drawn circles labelled light source and not a light source. Ask learners to place objects into the correct group.

By the end of the activity, learners will be clear about a wider range of light source and things that are not light sources.

⟩ **Practical guidance:** If you are lighting a candle, ensure that you have water or sand close by so that you can put it out. Mention this to learners so that they know there is potential danger.

⟩ **Differentiation ideas:** You might ask less confident learners to complete Worksheet 5.1A, which asks them to group light sources and not light sources. You might ask more confident learners to complete Worksheet 5.1C, which asks learners to explain why one thing is a light sources and another not a light source.

As learners are working and responding with answers or in activities, note any difficulties or signs of better understanding, so that in later activities you can support and challenge learners.

⟩ **Assessment ideas:** Ask a learner to suggest a light source found in different rooms in school for example, the office, a classroom, the school hall.

2 Activity 2: So many light sources
(20–30 minutes)

Learning intention: We are going to find different light sources, including the Sun.

We are going to find light sources powered by electricity.

We are going to record observations on a table.

Resources: Learner's Book, access to all or part of the school, copies of table in Learner's Book, Workbook 5.1 Practice and Challenge (optional), digital camera (optional)

Description: You might introduce this activity with discussion and completion of the Workbook 5.1 Practice exercise, which asks learners to consider whether several examples are or are not light sources. Read the description of the activity in the Learner's Book. Explain that we are going to look at different parts of the school in search of light sources. Ask learners to predict light sources they might see. It may be helpful for you to note objects observed and it might help to take digital photographs of objects observed. Now use the 'Science skills' section at the back of the Learner's Book. Read, with learners, the part called 'How to stay safe in the Sun'. This explains to learners why they should never look at the Sun.'

Begin the tour with an obvious light source, for example, a ceiling light and then an obvious non-light source, for example, a chair. From then, ask learners to identify objects and say whether they are, or are not, a light source. For example, a light, a screen, a warning light, an LED light on an alarm, an exit light, a polished floor, etc. Point out potentially challenging examples, for example, a mirror, a shiny surface, a window. When you return to class, ensure the record sheets are completed and several examples discussed. For example, 'Remember the mirror? What did we say about the mirror?'. Once again, refer to the Sun as an important source of light.

At this point, you could use the Workbook 5.1 Challenge activity, which encourages learners to think about the Moon, which is not a light source.

By the end of the activity, learners will have identified a range of light sources and objects that are not light sources.

> Practical guidance: You may or may not take the record sheets with you as you tour the school. Digital photographs make a very good record. Learners could group the photographs as light sources and non-light sources.

> Differentiation ideas: Support learners by pairing them with more confident learners.

Challenge some learners by asking, 'Are all light sources in school electrical?' (They may be because naked flames might be considered dangerous in a school.)

> Assessment ideas: You might use Workbook 5.1 Practice as an assessment at this point.

3 Think like a scientist: Which flashlight is brighter? (20–30 minutes)

Learning intention: We are going to find different light sources, including the Sun.

We are going to record observations on a table.

We are going to use given equipment to make observations.

Resources: Learner's Book, several different flashlights – at least three different ones per group/ pair of learners, small (approx. 10 cm × 10 cm) sheets of paper (four or five for each group/pair, copies of the record sheet (one per group), one poster-sized version of the record sheet (on paper of board)

Description: Read the description of the activity in the Learner's Book. Explain that different light sources shine differently. Some are brighter than others. This is true for flashlights which we can easily test for brightness by counting how many sheets of paper the light from each flashlight will shine through.

Tell them that we are going to answer a science question 'Which flashlight is brighter?'. Demonstrate holding a flashlight and one sheet of paper held up to the lamp. Can learners see that the light gets through? Ask a learner to add another sheet of the same paper and ask them to describe whether the light now gets through two sheets. Allow learners, in twos or threes, to try out the test with a flashlight and paper. Can they predict which flashlight is going to shine the brightest when turned on?

Ask them to work in their pairs or groups and plan what they will do. Ask them to draw what they will do on a separate sheet of paper. Ask a couple of groups to describe their plans. Check that they understand the record sheet. Show them how to complete it.

Ask learners to test first one flashlight and then another (making sure that they all use different flashlights on the second set of tests). If you have time, you might ask them to test a third flashlight.

Finally, ask them to talk together about, and then report, their results. Was the predicted flashlight the brightest? They should have proof from the test about which is the brightest flashlight. Point out that they have tested and compared the flashlights fairly and that they have proof that one is brighter then the other.

By the end of the activity, learners will understand that, whilst light sources vary in strength, they are all light sources. They will also have the opportunity to record results.

> Practical guidance: Try to have a range of flashlights available, including some which are less bright and others which are brighter. If you have around eight different flashlights, they could be shared by the groups. Check the paper you will use by trialling it. Very thin paper may need up to 10 sheets to block the light. This is too many. Try to find paper that needs 3–8 sheets to block all the light. Very thick paper or card will not give useful results.

> **Differentiation ideas:** Support less confident learners by providing sets of papers for them to test (two sheets stapled together, three sheets stapled together, and so on). Ask them to test flashlight strength by observing which flashlight shines through the most paper sheets.

Challenge more confident learners by asking them to design a different recording sheet. This can be challenging if they have not done it before. Start by asking them to improve the suggested table. For example, new boxes in the table to record the prediction and whether this was shown to be right or not.

> **Assessment ideas:** Can learners suggest a test to see which mobile phone screen is brightest?

Plenary ideas

1 Animals that glow (10 minutes)

Description: Learners may be interested to learn that some animals are light sources, for example, glow worms. Ask the learners if they have heard of other animals which glow (for example, some snails, some fish and some jellyfish). Ask learners to talk in pairs about why animals might do this (in some cases scientists don't know). This glowing is often used to lure prey to be eaten, or to attract a mate.

Learners may suggest that the light is to find things in the dark. This is not so, because most animals that are active at night have very good night vision.

> **Reflection ideas:** Ask learners about the many ways that animals are different. Is this a good thing?

2 Fluorescent materials are not light sources (10 minutes)

Resources: Highly reflective or fluorescent material, for example, piece of reflective fabric, flashlight, a jacket or coat

Description: Explain that many adults think that fluorescent materials are light sources because they are so bright. Ask a learner to shine the flashlight on the reflective or fluorescent fabric to show how it reflects light. Now put the fabric into a dark place, for example, into the sleeve of a jacket or coat. Ask a learner to look in the dark at the material. Ask them to report back to the class. Does it look bright? Repeat the demonstration with the flashlight to show that fluorescent material is not a light source.

> **Reflection ideas:** Ask learners if they would like to have fluorescent clothes. Why?

CROSS-CURRICULAR LINKS

When talking about fluorescent clothing, you can link this to personal, health and social education (PHSE) and road safety.

Homework ideas

Ask learners to draw two or three different light sources they find in their home. Remind them never to look at bright light sources.

Ask learners to talk to family members about the Moon. Do family members think this is a light source? Learners should explain that when we see the bright Moon shining, this light is from the Sun.

Topic worksheets

Worksheets 5.1A, 5.1B and 5.1C

Worksheet 5.1A asks learners to identify things as light sources or not light sources.

Worksheet 5.1B asks learners to group things as not light sources, light sources which are bright, and light sources which are not bright.

Worksheet 5.1C asks learners to say why some things are light sources and others not.

5.2 Darkness

Learning objectives	Learning intention	Success criteria
2Ps.02 Know that darkness is the absence of light.	• We are going to learn that with little or no light there is darkness.	• I can say that without light it is dark.
2TWSc.06 Collect and record observations and/or measurements by annotating images and completing simple tables.	• We are going to record observations on a table.	• I can record observations on a table.
2TWSa.02 Identify simple patterns in results.	• We are going to find patterns in our results.	• I can find patterns in my results.
1TWSc.04 Follow instructions safely when doing practical work.	• We are going to follow instructions safely when doing science.	• I can follow instructions safely when doing science.
2TWSp.02 Make predictions about what they think will happen.	• We are going to make predictions and see if they are right.	• I can make predictions and see if they are right.

LANGUAGE SUPPORT

We don't have as much language for darkness as we do for light as darkness is not useful to humans and we tend to sleep at night. However, most children are very interested in night time and darkness.

Make a poster of words we use at night, for example, night, night time, dark, darkness, take care, street light, glow, shine, Moon, stars.

Read a darkness or a night time related story to the class, for example, *The owl who was afraid of the dark, Funnybones.*

Ask learners to tell you their own stories of things they have done in the dark.

Talk to learners about darkness. They may be scared of the dark. Reassure them that there are no monsters, etc. However, they should take care, for example, when moving around in the dark.

dark: less light or no light

night time: the hours of darkness

Common misconceptions

Misconception	How to identify	How to overcome
Some learners may think darkness is the opposite of light not the absence of light.	You may notice this when you ask learners to talk about times when dark places become light and when light places become dark.	Show learners places that remain lit until a light source is removed.
Learners may talk about darkness as if it is something that spreads from corners and other dark places.	Ask learners about dawn and dusk. You may hear learners talk about darkness spreading out and moving back.	Show them a darkened place where you can add more and more light. Explain that, without light, there is darkness.
Some learners may be scared of the dark.	When talking about night time and bed time, learners may talk about fears.	Explain that darkness is just a lack of light. There are no monsters, etc. However, learners should take care moving around in the dark.

Starter ideas

1 Lights on at bedtime (5–10 minutes)

Resources: Learner's Book

Description: Look at the picture in the Learner's Book which shows Hafeez sitting in bed. Explain that, in order to sleep well, we need to sleep in the dark. Ask learners to tell you about bedtime and whether, when they are put to bed, there is any light or none at all. Ask them whether, when they are in bed, the room is dark but they can see dark shapes in the room.

(If any learners talk about fear of the dark, reassure them that there is nothing to fear, the room is the same as it is with the lights on, they should of course be careful if they have to move around a darkened room.) Make it clear that if the room is totally dark, they could see nothing, not even their own hand in front of their face. If anything can be seen, there is some light.

Some learners may find it difficult to realise that we use one word, dark, for a range of light levels. For most people, a dark place is one where, for example, reading starts to become difficult.

2 Can we see in the dark? (10 minutes)

Resources: Learner's Book, a large box or sheet of fabric, Workbook 5.2

Description: Ask learners to look at the picture showing a dark place in a classroom. Explain that we need light to see, just as now in class we can all see the room and one another. Show the learners a small tent you make (for example, drape fabric

over a chair on top of a table, or use a large box open at just one end). Place an open book inside. Ask a learner to take a look inside. Can they see? Can they see the book? Can they read the words? If they can, is it as easy as outside the tent? Explain that we do not often experience complete darkness, because there is often a light source giving a little light. So we call a place 'dark' even when there is a little light. Ask learners if it is completely dark at night in their bedroom. Do they know where the light comes from? Learners may be confused by the word 'dark' because we rarely experience complete darkness.

At this point you might use the Workbook 5.2 Focus section, which illustrates this activity.

Safety: Warn learners that it is easy to have an accident in dark places.

Main teaching ideas

1 Activity 1: Darkness in our classroom (20–30 minutes)

Learning intention: We are going to learn that with little or no light there is darkness.

Resources: Learner's Book, sticky labels, Workbook 5.2 Focus, Digital Classroom song: We can't see when the lights go out (optional), Worksheets 5.2A, 5.2B, 5.2C (optional)

Description: Read the description of the activity in the Learner's Book. Ask learners whether they know about, or can see, places in the classroom which will be dark or darker, for example, a corner away from the window, behind furniture. Ask one or two learners to suggest places and then to take a closer look to investigate and confirm if this place is darker than the main classroom area.

If the learners have books on their table, ask them to lift a book a little (about 1 cm) and peep under. Is it darker under the book?

Ask learners to talk in pairs and think of places in the room which might be quite dark. They may suggest: behind a cupboard, under a table, in a corner, inside a cupboard, drawer or closed tray. Try to accept as many suggestions as possible.

Ask learners to explain why these places are darker. They may talk about lack of light, perhaps saying there is no light, little light or no light source.

You could ask learners to complete the Focus section in the Workbook, if not done already, where learners are asked to predict whether different coloured things will be easy or hard to find in the dark.

You could write on a number of sticky labels: dark, quite dark and very dark. Ask learners to select appropriate labels and put them by the darker area, perhaps adding an arrow to point to the darker area.

By the end of the activity, learners should realise that they are surrounded by places which are dark and some even darker, places where there is little or no light.

Depending on the level of challenge required by learners, you could ask learners to discuss and complete Worksheet 5.2A, where they have to label a room light, dark, darker and darkest, Worksheet 5.2B where they have to explain why a room is light and at another times dark and even darker, or Worksheet 5.2C, where they have answer questions about the reasons for different light levels in a room.

⟩ **Digital Classroom:** If you have access to the Digital Classroom component, use the song 'We can't see when the lights go out' to finish the lesson with a song about why we need light. The i button will explain how to use the song.

⟩ **Practical guidance:** Warn learners that some dark places can be dangerous, and that they should never climb into a cupboard or anything with a door because they may get locked in.

⟩ **Differentiation ideas:** Less confident learners might be asked to complete Worksheet 5.2A, which asks for a judgement about a room and whether it is light, dark, darker and darkest. More confident learners might answer more challenging questions on Worksheet 5.2C.

⟩ **Assessment ideas:** You might use Workbook 5.2 Practice as an assessment of learners' understanding of our need for light when it is dark.

2 Activity 2: Using a dark box (30 minutes)

Learning intention: We are going to learn that with little or no light there is darkness.

We are going to follow instructions safely when doing science.

Resources: Learner's Book, boxes (around the size of shoes boxes, but other sizes will also work) each with a small hole in the side, different coloured objects, for example, white, black, yellow, green red and blue bricks or other coloured objects, scissors, Digital Classroom animation: Can you see in the dark? (optional)

Description: Read the description of the activity in the Learner's Book. Introduce the activity by looking at the picture in the Learner's Book. Explain that inside the closed box will be dark, we will peep in through the side. Ask learners to place a dark (black, red, blue) coloured object into the box, close the lid and peep inside. Ask them to predict whether they will see the object. Can learners see the object (it may be possible as a little light will get in)? Ask several class members about what they could see. Was it hard to see the object? Could they see the outline?

Now ask them to repeat the test with a light coloured object. Ask them to report whether this light coloured object was easier or harder to see than the dark coloured object.

By the end of the activity, learners will be clear that in darkness it is difficult to see.

⟩ **Digital Classroom:** If you have access to the Digital Classroom component, this may be a good place to use the animation 'Can you see in the dark?'. Use the animation to encourage learners to think about whether we can see in the dark. The i button will explain how to use the animation.

⟩ **Practical guidance:** Make the hole in the box for the learners. The hole in the side if the box should be 5 mm (approx.) in diameter. If the hole in the side of the box is too small, learners may not be able to see inside. If it is too big, it will let too much light in.

> Differentiation ideas: Support less confident learners by providing very obvious light and dark objects initially which can or cannot be seen easily.

Challenge learners by asking them to explain why things are hard to see in the dark box.

> Assessment ideas: Ask learners to talk about other times when they experience darkness. Is it a place where a light can be turned on/off for light and dark? Ask them to describe what happens.

3   Think like a scientist: How much light do I need to see? (30 minutes)

Learning intention: We are going to learn that with little or no light there is darkness.

We are going to record observations on a table.

We are going to make predictions and see if they were right.

We are going to identify patterns in our results.

Resources: Learner's Book, boxes (around the size of shoes boxes, but other sizes will also work) each with a small hole in the side and a flap in the top, different coloured objects, for example, white, black, yellow, green red and blue bricks or other coloured objects, scissors, copies of the record sheet as shown in the Learner's Book

Description: Read the description of the activity in the Learner's Book.

Show learners the boxes that they used in the previous activity, but that now have a small flap or door (approximately 6 cm × 4 cm) added to the lid (cut by an adult). Ask a learner to demonstrate putting a coloured object into the box, closing the lid and looking into the box through the small hole. Then ask them to open the lid a little (approximately 0.5 mm) and then a little more (approximately 1 cm) and then fully open, each time looking in the box at the object.

Check that learners understand how to do the experiment, show them the record sheet and ask them in pairs or threes to conduct the test, recording their observations.

After 10–15 minutes, ask one or two groups to report back on the observations.

By the end of the activity, learners will have a better understanding of levels of light needed to see things.

> Practical guidance: Cut the flap for the learners. An alternative option if the box has a lid is just to open the lid a little and then more.

Check that learners are clear about the gradual opening of the flap.

> Differentiation ideas: Support learners who find this challenging by reducing the number of objects and perhaps demonstrating the first test of one object.

Challenge others by adding a black coloured object, or by asking them to design their own table or results.

> Assessment ideas: Ask learners about objects they have looked for in the dark. Were some easier to find (for example, light coloured objects)? Could they find things in complete darkness (they could feel for them but their eyes would not help)?

Plenary ideas

1   Working in the dark (10 minutes)

Resources: Learner's Book, Workbook 5.2 Challenge

Description: Ask learners to look at the photo of people working underground in the Learner's Book in Topic 5.2, following Activity 2. Check that learners can see the lighting and the bright clothing with reflective strips. Ask learners to talk in pairs about working in the dark (at night or underground). What would it be like? Would it be safe? How can we make it safe? Ask a number of pairs to report back about their thoughts about working in the dark and about safety for these workers. At this point you might use the Workbook 5.2 Challenge exercise, which is about things we can see in darkness.

> Assessment ideas: Can learners talk about light sources used by their family outdoors at night?

> Reflection ideas: Ask learners about animals which have very good eyes for the night time, for example, owls. What would it be like if we could see very well at night?

2   Road safety (10 minutes)

Resources: A light coloured jacket

Description: Ask the learners about any dangers they face when they go out in the dark. Did they know that many people are badly hurt or killed by cars, buses and lorries each year in the dark? Explain that when it is dark, they should be with a grown up, but they can make themselves safer by choosing the right clothes. Ask the learners in pairs or threes to talk about the choices they could make to be safer in the dark.

> **Assessment ideas:** Ask learners about cars and motorbikes. How do the lights on the car or bike help the driver?

> **Reflection ideas:** Ask learners how they can help even younger children to be safe at night outside.

CROSS-CURRICULAR LINKS

You can link this topic to work on safety in PHSE lessons.

Homework ideas

Ask learners to test curtains or blinds tonight. If they hold a flashlight or mobile phone behind the curtain, does it let light through?

Ask learners to draw the view from their bedroom window just before bedtime. Is the Sun down? Is the Moon in the sky? Are there lights on?

Topic worksheets

Worksheets 5.2A, 5.2B and 5.2C

Worksheet 5.2A asks learners to label 4 rooms as light, dark, darker and darkest.

Worksheet 5.2B asks learners to explain why a room is light and at another times dark and even darker.

Worksheet 5.2C challenges learners to answer questions about the reasons for different light levels in a room.

5.3 The Sun appears to move!

LEARNING PLAN

Learning objectives	Learning intention	Success criteria
2ESs.01 Describe the apparent movement of the Sun during the day.	• We are going to investigate how the Sun seems to move during the day.	• I can investigate the way the Sun seems to move in the day.
2TWSm.03 Describe the difference between a diagram and a picture.	• We are going to talk about the difference between a picture and a diagram.	• I can talk about the difference between a picture and a diagram.
2TWSc.06 Collect and record observations and/or measurements by annotating images and completing simple tables.	• We are going to draw and label a diagram. • We are going to collect and record observations.	• I can draw and label a diagram. • I can collect and record observations.
2TWSa.02 Identify simple patterns in results	• We are going to look for patterns in results.	• I can find patterns in results.
2TWSc.04 Follow instructions safely when doing practical work.	• We are going to follow instructions safely when doing practical work.	• I can follow instructions safely when doing practical work.

LANGUAGE SUPPORT

This topic is normally of great interest to learners. The ideas and words may, however, be unfamiliar.

Give the learners lots of opportunity to talk in these lessons because this will help them develop their ideas.

Use 'snowballing', that is, ask learners to talk in pairs, then join pairs to talk in groups of four, before returning to whole class discussion.

Show that you value learners' questions by:

- providing a poster for these questions, demonstrate question asking behaviour, posing a question yourself and adding it to the poster.

- Display poster-sized version of learners' tables of results and label them. For example, here is the pattern, can you see …?

daylight: the light we get from the Sun

position: an object's place in the physical world

star: a very large burning object in the sky which is very far away and so appears very small

Common misconceptions

Misconception	How to identify	How to overcome
Learners may think that the Sun actually moves.	When observing the Sun, learners may talk about the moving Sun.	Whilst the concept of the Earth spinning being the reason why the Sun appears to move is beyond the Stage 2 curriculum, it is important to explain this if a learner expresses the view that the Sun actually moves.
		Borrow an office chair that spins and ask the child to sit on it and to keep their head still. Hold a ball to represent the Sun. Slowly turn the seat of the chair and learner. Keeping their head still, can the learner see the ball appear to move?

Starter ideas

1 Have you seen the Sun appear to move? (5 minutes)

Resources: A yellow disc of paper or card

Description: Ask learners about the different times of the day they might notice the Sun e.g. early morning, anytime in the day. Have they noticed how its position change during the day? How at some times it appears low in the sky and other times high in the sky?

Ask a learner to hold the yellow disc low, close to the floor. Ask another learner to take the disc and hold it very high. Explain that this is a model to show different positions of the Sun in the day (DO NOT ask one learner to hold and move the disc in the 'sky' as this would reinforce the misconception that the Sun moves). Ask learners whether they have noticed a pattern in the way the Sun's position changes in the sky each day (e.g it appears low in the morning, appears high at midday and then appears low in the evening.

2 Where will the Sun appear next? (10 minutes)

Resources: Learner's Book

Description: Ask learners to look at the picture of the house at the start of Topic 5.3.

Ask them to talk in pairs and report back about what they notice, for example, a clear sky, a house, a dark garden, a light on in the house, no Sun in the sky, no stars, brightness low in the sky.

Explain that the photograph was taken at the end of the day. There is still plenty of light outside the house. Ask learners to talk about the coming hours and how things will change. Ask them about the amount of light outside and inside the house. Would they see any lights in the sky? e.g. aeroplanes, stars (note that the Moon in not a light source).

Teaching that the apparent movement of the Sun is caused by the Earth spinning is a Stage 4 learning objective. It can be taught here as extension material if learners refer to the Sun physically moving in the sky.

Main teaching ideas

1 Activity: Looking at patterns (20–30 minutes)

Learning intention: We will investigate how the Sun seems to move during the day.

We will talk about the difference between a diagram and a picture.

We will collect and record observations.

We will look for patterns in results.

Resources: Learner's Book, Workbook 5.3 Focus activity, a space outdoors where learners can observe the sky (if you cannot go outside then a large window may be enough), Worksheet 5.3A, B or C (optional)

Before starting this activity, use the 'Science skills' section at the back of the Learner's Book. Read, with learners, the part called 'How to stay safe in the Sun'. This explains to learners why they should never look at the Sun.

Read the description of the activity in the Learner's Book.

Find a place where learners can observe where the Sun is in the sky (warn them not to look directly at it). Initially ask them to draw the view with at least one object on the ground, for example, a tree, a shrub, a wall or building. Make several observations at perhaps 10am, 11am, 12 noon, 1pm, 2pm. adding the new position of Sun each time in relation to the first drawing. Three, but ideally four or more, observations will be enough. Learners should have a diagram developing during the day with the Sun appearing at different places at different times. Check that learners notice the Sun appears higher around midday. Do learners notice a pattern?

At this point you may wish to use Worksheet 5.3A, 5.3B or 5.3C. Worksheet 5.3A asks learners to draw the position of the Sun at several times in a day. Worksheet 5.3B asks learners to read times on clock faces and then draw the position of the Sun at these times of the day. They then finish a sentence about the apparent movement of the Sun. Worksheet 5.3C asks the learner to draw seveal times onto clock faces and then draw the Sun's position at these times of day. Learners then finish a sentence about the pattern seen in the apparent movement of the Sun. By the end of this activity learners should be clearer about the way that the Sun appears to move across the sky during the day.

> **Practical guidance:** You will need at least three observations.

> **Differentiation ideas:** Challenge more confident learners to look at their results and use them to say where the Sun appear be after school closes. For less confident learners ask them if they would expect the pattern to be repeated tomorrow?

> **Assessment ideas:** After their final drawing, ask a learner to point to or draw where the Sun will be in the morning tomorrow.

2 Think like a scientist: Showing the way the Sun appears to move (30 minutes)

Learning intention We are going to investigate how the Sun appears to move during the day..

Resources: Learners Book, card, coloured crayons, a magnet, a paper clip, sticky tape

Description: Ask learners to read the description of the activity. Remind learners about keeping safe by reading 'How to stay safe in the Sun', in the science skills section of the Learners Book.

Explain that in science we often make and use models to help us understand how things happen. This model will help us understand the movement of the Sun in the daytime.

Remind learners that in Stage 1 they learned about magnets and the materials that are magnetic (attracted to magnets). Explain that we can make a picture with moving parts controlled by a magnet. Ask them in pairs to design and draw a picture with trees, buildings and a lot of sky, like the one in the Learners Book.

Ask them to cut a circle of paper or card which they should colour yellow and stick on the back of it the metal paper clip.

They can now use the magnet to control the movement of the model Sun to that its position changes in the picture. They should follow a curved path starting low on the left, rising higher and then appearing low on the right (models the east to west appearance in the northern hemisphere, if you are in the southern hemisphere they should start on the right and move the model left.).

Explain that they will learn more in later stages about why the Sun appears to move. If learners ask you can, as extension learning, mention that the Sun is still and it is the spin of the earth which causes this affect.

Explain that this is a model and so it is not perfect. For example on the model the Sun appears to crash into the Earth at the end of the day. You might set a challenge to see if learners can change the model so that the Sun's position moves behind a house or tree.

> **Assessment ideas:** Ask learners to move the Sun to show how it would appear early in the morning, at lunchtime and at the end of school.

Plenary ideas

1 If I am planet Earth I can see the Sun appear to move (extension activity) (10 minutes)

Description: This extension activity can be used where learners have raised the question about whether the Sun moves or not. Ask two children to stand side by side. Ask one to smile, he/she represents the (shining) Sun and must stay still. Ask the other learner to represent 'planet Earth' and, without moving their feet or turning, to point to the 'Sun' and say 'the Sun is on my right/left'. Now ask the 'Earth' child to slowly, on the spot, move their feet and turn anti-clockwise.' After 5–10 seconds, ask the 'Earth' learner to stop and say where the Sun is now. Ask, is the Sun in the same place as at the start? Does it appear to have moved for you? Ask this learner to keep turning until the Sun is on the other side. Ask them to stop and ask, 'is the Sun still on your right/left had side as it was at the start? It should now be on the other side. At the end of this activity, learners should see that the Sun does not move but, if we spin, the Sun will appear to move.

> **Assessment ideas:** Ask other learners to watch the demonstration. Can they then repeat it or give instructions to two other learners?

> **Reflection ideas:** How does an activity like this help you learn?

2 Confused Hiba! (10 minutes)

Resources: a globe, a flashlight

Description: This challenge activity can be used where learners have raised the question about whether the Sun moves. Explain that your friend Hiba is a teacher and has to explain to her class how the Sun's position appears to change in the sky each day. Ask your class to suggest how Hiba can explain this using the globe and the flashlight.

> **Assessment ideas:** Ask learners to pretend that they are presenting a radio report about the Sun. Can they describe to listeners how the Sun's position appears to change in the sky each day? Can they use the word pattern?

> **Reflection ideas:** Ask if they have ever been confused? Does it help to have people listen to you and then explain ideas? Why does this help?

CROSS-CURRICULAR LINKS

This topic links to mathematics as we are talking about time.

Homework ideas

Ask learners to keep a light diary at home. Can they list and draw three or more different light sources used after they get home, starting with: the Sun … (they might add, kitchen light, TV, phone, bedroom light, bathroom light, the Moon etc).

Ask learners to make a note or draw the position of the Sun at home in the morning, for example, the Sun shines in at the back door. Following this, a note or drawing of the Sun's position at the end of the day, for example, it appears on the other side of the house shining into the kitchen.

Topic worksheets

Worksheets 5.3A, 5.3B and 5.3C

In Worksheet 5.3A, learners draw the Sun at different times given in words. It provides a prompt with the Sun drawn in at 12 o'clock.

Worksheet 5.3B gives the times on clock faces. This sheet also asks for a sentence about the pattern of the Sun's apparent movement.

Worksheet 5.3C asks learners to draw the times on the clock faces, draw the Sun's position at these times and describe the pattern of the Sun in the sky.

PROJECT: MY BOOK OF LIGHT

2SIC.01 Talk about how some of the scientific knowledge and thinking now was different in the past.

Learners are asked to prepare a book (or poster) about light in a similar way to Issac Newton's book 'Opticks' from 1704. You might talk about Newton, who was born in a small English village, but who was very curious, asked many questions and loved mathematics and science. He became a very famous scientist. One interest of Newton's was light. He made many discoveries, including how white light is made up of the colours of the spectrum. Explain that Newton improved our understanding of light, and that other scientists have improved on his ideas since then. For example, we now know the speed that light travels at.

Encourage learners to write short section with illustrations on: Issac Newton, light sources, things that are not light sources, darkness. They might choose other things to include from the Learner's Book, for example, tests using the dark box, light from the Sun, day and night, fluorescent materials, etc.

Encourage them to use as many science words as possible.

Encourage learners to title the book including their name, for example, Hatif's Book of Light.

Assist your learners by making books, posters and pictures available as well as access to the internet.

>6 Electricity

Unit plan

Topic	Approximate number of learning hours	Outline of learning content	Resources
6.1 Where do we use electricity?	2	This topic is the basis for the unit. This is opportunity for learners to observe, talk about and research the ways we use electricity. They are asked to look around school at the various electrical appliances. The danger of mains electricity is stressed. They are asked to look at different features of electrical equipment including switches.	**Learner's Book:** Activity 1: Electricity in school Activity 2: Which switch? Think like a scientist: Finding out about electricity **Workbook:** Topic 6.1 **Teacher's Resource:** ⬇ Worksheets 6.1A, 6.1B, 6.1C **Digital Classroom:** Song – There's electricity
6.2 Keep safe with electricity	2	In this topic learners will explore and learn about the dangers of electricity. A basic set of rules will be established which will keep learners safe.	**Learner's Book:** Activity 1: Mains means danger Activity 2: Electrical safety poster Think like a scientist: Electrical safety survey **Workbook:** Topic 6.2 **Teacher's Resource:** ⬇ Worksheets 6.2A, 6.2B, 6.2C
6.3 Making circuits	2	In this topic learners will become familiar with cells, wires, lamps and lamp holders and how these can be used to make several working circuits.	**Learner's Book:** Activity 1: Make a circuit Think like a scientist: Do more lamps mean brighter lamps? Activity 2: Why are wires made of metal? Activity 3: Do more cells make lamps brighter?

Topic	Approximate number of learning hours	Outline of learning content	Resources
			Workbook: Topic 6.3
			Teacher's Resource:
			⬇ Worksheets 6.3A, 6.3B, 6.3C
			Digital Classroom:
			Manipulative – Can you build a circuit?

Across Unit resources

Learner's Book:

Project: Invent a new electrical appliance

Check your progress quiz

Teacher's Resource:

⬇ Language worksheets 1 and 2

⬇ Diagnostic check

Digital Classroom:

⬇ End-of-unit quiz

BACKGROUND KNOWLEDGE

You need to be able to recognise common electrical appliances found in homes and in school. This should include mains appliances, for example, TVs, kettles, fans, etc, and cell-powered appliances, for example, phones, flashlights, remote controls, etc. A very important message in this topic is about electrical safety. You will need to talk about potential dangers from: water, dust and dirt, wires and cables, overloading wall sockets, damaged appliances. Refer to the importance of electrical safety in most lessons in this unit. If parents express any concern, explain that you are teaching about electrical safety and that you mention it in every lesson in this topic.

A cell is a source of electricity. When we put two or more cells together, we call it a battery. Use shop-bought 1.5 V cells, but not rechargeable cells because these can overheat. You can use a cell holder to connect a cell to a circuit, or you can hold wires in place.

Make sure the voltage of the cell in a circuit is not bigger than the voltage marked on the lamp. If the voltage is too high it will break the tiny wire in the lamp, this is not dangerous to learners. If this happens, make sure you dispose of the lamp safely because it is made of glass.

To test that a lamp is working use a cell and one wire as below.

CONTINUED

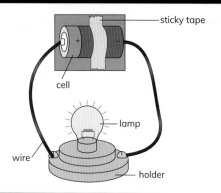

If you don't have cell holders and learners have difficulty holding the cell still whilst they construct circuits, try using sticky tape to hold the cell to a piece of card as shown. Learners will then find it much easier. Crocodile clips are ideal, but not essential. They make it easy to clip wires onto lamp holders and cell holders. Cell holders are a great help when making circuits, but they are not essential. When using the lamp holders, an electrical screwdriver can be helpful, but they are not essential.

TEACHING SKILLS FOCUS

Language awareness

Mixed methods

There is some new and unfamiliar language to learn in this unit, so use a mix of role play, hands on activity, posters and books. These will assist with the introduction of, and practice of, the new terms. As well as demonstrating science terms yourself, use activities to encourage learners to talk and use the language of electricity.

Active learning

Making and breaking circuits

Try to ensure time and resources for as much circuit making as possible. Ask learners to take circuits apart and remake them. Encourage learners to ask questions about circuits. Here are some examples. Does turning the cell around make a difference? (it won't) Does turning the lamp around make a difference? (it won't)

Encourage exploration and prediction

When making circuits, allow learners to trial different numbers of cells and lamps in different combinations. As often as possible, ask learners to predict whether they think a circuit will work.

Fault finding

Encourage learners to try to find the fault if a circuit does not work. For example, try to replace the cell, replace the lamp, check whether all connections are made.

Cross curricular learning

Link this topic to other learning about health and safety as you talk to learners about, and ask learners to talk about, electrical safety. There are also links to history in the development of electricity, discoveries and the uses we make of electricity.

6.1 Where do we use electricity?

Learning objectives	Learning intention	Success criteria
2Pe.01 Identify how we use electricity and describe how to be safe with it.	• We are going to investigate different ways we use electricity.	• I can investigate different ways we use electricity.
2TWSc.01 Sort and group objects, materials and living things based on observations of the similarities and differences between them.	• We are going to sort and group different types of switches.	• I can sort and group different types of switches.
2TWSc.05 Use a given secondary information source to find an answer to a question.	• We are going to find the answer to questions using books and the internet.	• I can find the answer to questions using books and the internet.

LANGUAGE SUPPORT

This topic includes some familiar language when learners talk about electrical appliances they use, but there is also unfamiliar language about, for example, electrical components, for example, lamp, lamp holder.

Provide a poster with pictures cut out from magazines and catalogues to record electrical appliances, for example, flashlights, calculator, mobile phones, toys, etc.

Make a hands-on display with electrical components labelled. Allow learners to play at 'inventing circuits'. Ask them to name circuits for example, 'the one cell, one lamp circuit'.

Ask learners to set aside an electricity glossary page in their science book. Have them keep returning to this page to add words and their definitions.

Model words very clearly, ask learners to watch your lips and tongue as you say, for example, electricity, ask them to repeat it back to you.

Language worksheets 1 and 2 are provided to assist learners with science vocabulary. As well as completing the sentences in Language worksheet 2, these worksheets can be used in different ways. They can be used as:

• posters on the classroom wall

• a glossary in learners' books

• as a prompt sheet on a learner's desk

• in a classroom display

• words and pictures can be cut out and used in a matching game, for example, can you match the word or sentence to the picture?

cell (electrical): a source of electricity

dangerous: it may hurt you

discovery: something found for the first time

electrical appliance: a device that uses electricity to work

electricity: we use it to make things work like TVs, computers, phones

CONTINUED

invention: something new created by a person

mains electricity: very powerful electricity we use in buildings

plug: a connection to mains electricity

power station: a factory that makes electricity

robot: an appliance that can do things by following instructions

rocked: something that moves from side to side

slide: to move something from side to side

store: a place where something is kept to use later

switch: a device to control the flow of electricity (on/off)

wire: a long thin piece of metal

Common misconceptions

Misconception	How to identify	How to overcome
Some learners may consider that non-electrical items use electricity, for example, a clockwork clock.	This may occur in discussion about electrical and other things we use.	Make it clear that the item does not have cells and is not plugged in.

Starter ideas

1 Electricity I use each day (10–15 minutes)

Resources: Worksheet 6.1A, 6.1B, 6.1C (optional), scissors

Description: Ask the learners to tell you about the first electrical thing they used today. For example, a light, a toothbrush, air conditioning, radio, TV. Then ask them to talk in pairs about what these things do and other things they have used today. Ask for learners to report back. This should give many examples of different electrical devices. These might include computers, tablets, lights, radio, music players, electricity in a car or bus, mobile phone, etc.

Misconceptions may be revealed: for example, learners may refer to non-electrical items, for example, a water tap. Point out that these do not have wires or cells, water is pushed out by water in the pipes.

You might make use of Worksheet 6.1A, 6.1B, or 6.1C to support this activity.

Worksheet 6.1A asks learners to circle the things that use electricity. It then asks them to cut out the pictures and arrange them into two groups: things that use electricity and things that do not use electricity.

Worksheet 6.1B also asks learners to circle the things that use electricity and that don't use electricity. It then asks learners to cut out the pictures and arrange them into three groups: things that use mains electricity, things that use cells and things that do not use electricity.

Worksheet 6.1C asks learners to circle those things that use electricity and asks them to explain what the electricity makes the machine do. For example, the electricity in a smart phone makes the sound of the voice of the other person, it also sends your voice to the other person, it also makes sound and even may take a photograph.

2 What do we know about electricity? (10 minutes)

Resources: Learner's Book

Description: Ask learners to tell you things they know about electricity. Give them two minutes to talk in pairs about this. Then ask them to tell you about what they know. This might include: electrical dangers, electrical safety, how electricity is made, power cables, cells or batteries. They might use terms like volt, or talk about workers they have seen working on electrical systems. Use this opportunity to let them talk so that you learn about what they know. Listen carefully to what learners say as they may reveal misconceptions that need to be corrected.

If you have time, ask them to look at the photograph in this topic of the power station. Ask them what they see and what they think this is. Explain that this is a power station where powerful mains electricity is made. Ask if they can see a building, wires and cooling towers. Explain that power stations can be dangerous places and only people who work there should go near them.

Main teaching ideas

1 Activity 1: Electricity in school (40 minutes)

Learning intention: We are going to investigate different ways we use electricity.

Resources: Learner's Book, access to part of the school, Workbook 6.1 Focus and practice (optional), Digital Classroom song: There's electricity (optional)

Description: You might use the Workbook 6.1 Focus exercise to start lesson as it will indicate learner confidence to identify electrical appliances.

Take the learners for a walk around part of the school. Ask them to look out for appliances powered by electricity, for example, door bells, alarms, lights, signs, computers, TVs, air conditioning, kettles, etc. Ask learners to explain why they think things are powered by electricity. Take note of any learners pointing out non-electrical items as electrical, for example, hot water pipes, heating radiators. Explain that these do not have wires or cells, that they are not electrical.

Ask learners to say whether each item is powered from the mains or in powered from cells, or whether they are not sure. By the end of this activity, learners should be able to recall a number of appliances which use electricity.

> **Digital Classroom:** If you have access to the Digital Classroom component you might at this point use the song 'There's electricity', which introduces ideas about electricity and associated vocabulary. The i button will explain how to use the song.

You might use the Workbook 6.1 Practice exercise to conclude the lesson as it will indicate the learners' level of confidence with the use by appliances of cells and mains electricity.

> **Practical guidance:** You might take digital photographs of electrical appliances to show back in class.

> **Assessment ideas:** Can learners draw two or more appliances that use electricity?

2 Activity 2: Which switch? (20–30 minutes)

Learning intentions: We are going to investigate different ways we use electricity.

We are going to sort and group different types of switches.

Resources: Learner's Book, several appliances (or photographs of appliances) that are powered by cells or batteries and which have different types of switches, for example, calculator, cell-powered computer keyboard or TV remote (each button is a switch), different flashlights, toys, cell-powered fan, toothbrush, screwdriver, etc., label cards for each type of switch: push switches, rocker switches and sliding switches (have a spare card for another switch you might find), copies of a table like the one in the Learner's Book

Description: Introduce (if possible) real examples of cell-powered and battery-powered appliances. Asking one or two learners to demonstrate the switching on and off of these appliances. Ask them to repeat and explain what they are doing, explaining how the switch works. Does it press, rock or slide? They might notice that some switches are very easy to press, that others are harder and that some switches 'click' on and off and stay on or off.

Explain that they can only handle appliances powered by cells in this activity because they are safer than mains-powered appliances.

Ask the learners to sort the appliances into groups based on the type of switch. Ask learners to use a table like the one in the Learner's Book.

Learners may need to experience a range of switches to understand that they are all switches. By the end of this activity, learners should be more aware of switches and that there are different types of switch.

> **Practical guidance:** It is much better here for learners to experience the switches physically, so if you are using photographs, try to provide some physical examples as well.

Tablet computers and smart phones don't have mechanical switches. They use a sensitive screen, not switches.

> **Assessment ideas:** Can learners describe two different types of switch? Can they move like a switch to on and off?

3 Think like a scientist: Finding out about electricity (40 minutes)

Learning intention: We are going to investigate different ways we use electricity.

We are going to find the answer to questions using books and the internet.

Resources: Learner's Book, books about electricity its discovery, and the inventions of electrical appliances and devices, books about scientists and inventors, poster paper, access to the internet, Workbook 6.1 Challenge

Description: Explain to learners that electricity is an important part of science and that lots of scientists and inventors have helped to make the appliances we use today. At this point, you might ask learners to complete the Workbook 6.1 Challenge exercise, which is about Thomas Edison's invention of the electric light bulb.

Ask learners to look at the Learner's Book and, in this topic, the picture of Michael Faraday. Ask the class to work in pairs and to find out more about electricity and about the people who discovered how to use it. Ask them all to include Michael Faraday (who discovered many features of electricity) or Thomas Edison (who invented things that use electricity, for example, the electric light bulb). Ask learners to present what they find on a poster.

If learners are using the Internet, remind them how to use it safely by reading 'Staying Safe on the Internet' in the 'Science skills' section at the back of the Learner's Book.

By the end of this activity, learners should be able to talk about information they have found.

> **Practical guidance:** Some learners may need more guidance and support. For example, show

them how to use the contents list in a book to find information, suggest words to search for on the internet, check spellings, search engines to use.

> **Differentiation ideas:** Assist less confident learners by giving them headings to research, for example, Thomas Edison's Electric Light.

More confident learners might research other people or topics, such as Benjamin Franklin, the ancient Greeks, batteries, electricity in the home, power plants, static electricity.

> **Assessment ideas:** Ask learners to write or draw pictures to show new information they have found.

Plenary ideas

1 Electricity in space (10–15 minutes)

Resources: Learner's Book

Description: Explain that, for people living and working in space, electricity is very useful.

Ask learners to look at the picture of the Mars Curiosity Rover at the start of this topic and look at the wheels, which are all powered by electricity, and the arms and camera box which move, powered by electricity. Can they suggest other appliances in the rover which will be powered by electricity? (For example, radio, thermometer, light, shovel, etc.)

Have learners heard that there are plans to send more people into space? To the space station, the Moon and to Mars?

Ask learners to talk about, and then report back about, their ideas on different ways that astronauts might use electricity. (Prompts: to cook, exercise, do experiments (for example, grow plants), space walk, play games, listen to music, use a radio, read a book, go to the toilet, etc.)

> **Assessment ideas:** Can learners suggest (talk about, write or draw) ways that astronauts might use electricity?

> **Reflection ideas:** Ask learners: why do humans like to explore places?

2 Places without electricity (10 minutes)

Description: Ask the learners about places where people live, but maybe without electricity. For example, in deep jungles, up high mountains, in some frozen places.

Ask them to imagine a life without electricity. Ask them to talk in groups of four about how that would live for a day without electricity. What would they do?

> **Assessment ideas:** Can learners talk about the things we use electricity for, which they would have to do without?

> **Reflection ideas:** Ask learners whether and why people can be happy without electricity.

CROSS-CURRICULAR LINKS

Link this topic to other learning about health and safety as you talk to learners about, and ask learners to talk about, electrical safety. There are also links to history in the development of electricity, discoveries and the uses we make of electricity.

Homework Ideas

Ask learners to draw two electrical appliances at home. Ask them to say whether they use cells or mains and what the appliance does.

Ask learners to ask a family member 'what are your two favourite electrical appliances?'. Learners should draw the appliances and the family member using them.

Topic worksheets

Worksheets 6.1A, 6.1B and 6.1C

Worksheet 6.1A asks learners to circle the things that use electricity. It then asks learners to cut out the pictures and arrange them into two groups: things that use electricity and things that do not use electricity.

Worksheet 6.1B also asks learners to circle the things that use electricity and that don't use electricity. It then asks learners to cut out the pictures and arrange them into three groups: things that use mains electricity, things that use cells and things that do not use electricity.

Worksheet 6.1C asks learners to circle those things that use electricity and asks them to explain what the electricity makes the machine do. For example, the electricity in a smart phone makes the sound of the voice of the other person, it also sends your voice to the other person, it also makes sound and even may take a photograph.

6.2 Keep safe with electricity

LEARNING PLAN

Learning objectives	Learning intention	Success criteria
2Pe.01 Identify how we use electricity and describe how to be safe with it.	• We are going to find out about how to keep safe with electricity.	• I can say how to keep safe with electricity.
2TWSc.06 Collect and record observations and/or measurements by annotating images and completing simple tables.	• We are going collect observations and write them in a table.	• I can collect observations and write them in a table.
2TWSp.02 Make predictions about what they think will happen.	• We are going to make predictions about what we think will happen.	• I can make predictions about what I think will happen.

LANGUAGE SUPPORT

Electrical safety is very important and should feature in all lessons in this topic. It is an important feature to talk about. Encourage learners to talk about safe ways to approach electricity.

Contact your local electricity supplier for posters about electrical safety. Use these in the classroom to emphasise language about electrical safety.

Use a puppet to 'talk' to the learners about electricity and how we use it.

Identify local danger spots for electricity, for example, power lines, electric railways, substations etc.

Ask learners to write and make safety posters for each spot.

Ask learners to write an electricity safety quiz. They could challenge learners or family members to complete the quiz.

Ask learners to make a digital audio recording of electricity safety rules to play to other learners.

electric shock: a dangerous amount of electricity in a person's body

protect: to take care of something or someone

safe: not dangerous

wall socket: the place you connect some electrical appliances to the mains

Common misconceptions

Misconception	How to identify	How to overcome
Some learners may be fearful and think that all electrical appliances are very dangerous and that they must not touch anything.	Ask learners to talk about electrical items they can and cannot handle.	Show the learners hand held devices powered by cells and explain that these are designed for people to handle. As long as they follow the rules, they will be safe.

Starter ideas

1 Danger around the home (10–15 minutes)

Resources: Learner's Book

Description: Ask learners to look at the first picture of this topic. Ask learners whether this child is in danger (yes). Following learners' response, ask them to talk in pairs about how we could make the child safer. For example, an adult could unplug and remove the appliances, an adult could put socket covers on the wall socket, we could explain to the child that she should never ever touch plugs and wires.

Ask the learners to look at the picture in the Learner's Book of the damaged wire. Ask learners whether they have ever seen something like this. Did learners know this is very dangerous because electricity can burn and even kill you? Electrical wire should always have a plastic cover to protect us. If learners see a damaged wire, they should step away, warn others and tell an adult.

Learners may have misconceptions about electrical safety. For example, that if they are in the home, electricity is safe.

2 Power lines (5–10 minutes)

Resources: Learner's Book

Description: Ask learners to look at the picture of the power station in the Learner's Book (Topic 6.1). Can they see the wires high up? These are high so that no one can touch them, they have a lot of electricity and are very dangerous. Can learners tell you where they see wires like this near to the school or home?

Explain that only electricity workers can go near these. All other people should keep well away because of the danger. They should keep away from any other poles, wire and equipment of the electricity company as they are so often very dangerous.

Learners may not realise how dangerous mains electricity can be. Alternatively, they may be scared of anything electrical.

Main teaching ideas

1 Activity 1: Mains means danger (20–30 minutes)

Learning intention: We are going to find out about how to keep safe with electricity.

Resources: Learner's Book, an unplugged mains appliance, for example, a kettle, a hair dryer, Workbook 6.2 Focus (optional), Worksheet 6.2A, 6.2B, 6.2C (optional)

Description: You might start the lesson with the Workbook 6.2 Focus exercise, which asks learners to circle electrical dangers in a classroom. Show the learners a mains-powered appliance. Tell them that it is unplugged and safe for an adult to hold and move. Ask them to observe the on/off switch, the electrical lead or wire and the mains plug. Explain that these are all things they should not touch.

Ask learners to look at the illustrations to do with electrical safety in the Learner's Book, for example, not putting things in wall sockets, keeping water away from electricity.

You might use Worksheet 6.2 to provide a differentiated activity about electrical dangers in the bathroom. Worksheet 6.2A asks learners to circle dangers, Worksheet 6.2B asks the learner to write a list of rules for electrical safety and Worksheet 6.2C asks learners to suggest other potential dangers.

Ask learners to work with a friend and write a set of rules for children to follow.

In the conclusion, make sure the class have covered the six rules in the Learner's Book.

It might assist learners to make use of Worksheet 6.2B, which asks for electrical safety rules in the bathroom.

> **Differentiation ideas:** Support less confident learners with Worksheet 6.2A and challenge the more confident learners with Worksheet 6.2B or or Worksheet 6.2C. You could also support less confident learners with prompts, for example, mains appliances, wires or plugs, wall sockets, water, dirt, damaged wire.

> **Assessment ideas:** Can learners tell you why mains electricity cables are often hidden in the walls of houses and other buildings?

2 Activity 2: Electrical safety poster (30–40 minutes)

Learning intention: We are going to learn about how to keep safe with electricity.

Resources: Learner's Book, Workbook 6.2 Practice and Challenge (optional)

Description: Together with the learners, look at the Learner's Book and this topic, which mentions some important formation for electrical safety. Review the six rules from the Learner's Book. You might use the Workbook 6.2 Practice exercise at this point. This asks learners to recognise electrical safety linked to wall sockets, water and damaged wires.

Ask learners in pairs, or threes, to design and make an electrical safety poster for children, one you could put up in school so that all the school learners will be safer. It must be one which will catch children's attention and convey the need for care around electrical appliances. You might conclude this activity with the Workbook 6.2 Challenge exercise which encourages discussion of electrical safety.

By the end of this activity, learners should be able to talk more confidently about electrical safety.

> **Assessment ideas:** Have learners written or drawn about two or more dangers of electricity?

3 Think like a scientist: Electrical safety survey (30–40 minutes)

Learning intention: We are going to learn about how to keep safe with electricity.

We are going to collect observations in a table.

Resources: Learner's Book, copies of table as shown in Learner's Book

Description: Explain that you want learners to find out if other learners in the school understand about electrical safety. You might use, change or adapt these questions from the Learner's Book.

1   Are children allowed to plug things in to a mains wall socket?
2   Should you touch an electrical appliance with wet hands?
3   Should we keep electrical things clean?
4   Can electricity hurt you?

Show the learners the table in the Learner's Book and explain that they can use this to tally the answer from 8–15 learners. You can arrange with another teacher that your class will visit them, or the survey could be done at break time, or the record sheet could be given to teachers who would ask their classes and return the results (try to have two or three of your learners present when this is done, so they can observe and report back to class). Ask learners to look at the results in the table and report what they see to you and the class. Look out for any answers which indicate confusion or misconceptions in the learners surveyed.

Ask learners to discuss again what these results tell them. Here are some examples of questions to ask.

- Are most learners safe?

- Are most learners in danger?

- Are some learners in danger?

Ask them what action we can now take, for example, providing posters, a set of rules, asking the teacher to explain to the children. By the end of this activity, learners should be confident to talk about electrical safety.

> **Practical guidance:** Ideally your learners need results from between 15 and 40 learners.

> **Differentiation ideas:** Support less confident learners by providing access to learners to survey just two at a time.

Challenge more confident learners to survey two groups, for example, younger and older learners.

> **Assessment ideas:** Can each learner advise another person about electrical safety?

Plenary ideas

1 Take care in the bathroom (10–15 minutes)

Resources: Worksheet 6.2A, 6.2B, 6.2C (if not already done)

Description: Introduce this idea by saying that bathrooms are dangerous places to use mains powered electrical appliances, because there is so much water. Have learners noticed that the light switch for a bathroom is often outside the room? Why is this? Have learners noticed that there is rarely a mains socket in a bathroom? Why is this?

Ask learners to complete Worksheet 6.2A, 6.2B or 6.2C which illustrates electrical danger in the

bathroom. Choose the worksheet that you feel suits their confidence with this topic.

In Worksheet 6.2A, learners circle the dangers.

For Worksheet 6.2B, learners write safety rules for electricity in the bathroom.

On Worksheet 6.2C, learners imagine and draw additional electrical dangers in the bathroom.

Make it clear that we should not use mains electrical appliances in the bathroom.

> **Assessment ideas:** Ask learners to present the ideas of their completed worksheet to another.

> **Reflection ideas:** Ask learners to think of life for people in the past who did not have electrical appliances in the home or hot tap water. What would bath time be like then?

2 Electricity at work (10–15 minutes)

Description: Ask learners to tell you what their parents do for a job, for example, shopkeeper, driver, nurse, teacher, etc. Ask them all to think about one job, or assign different jobs to different pairs. Give pairs two to three minutes to consider how this person uses electricity in their job, for example, computers, lights, vehicles. Ask different learners to report back on their thoughts.

> **Assessment ideas:** Play bounce the ball, use a real or imaginary ball. Throw it to one learner who has to refer to on safety rule for using electricity before throwing it to another learner.

> **Reflection ideas:** Ask learners about people at home. Whose job is it so stay safe with electricity?

CROSS-CURRICULAR LINKS

Link this topic to other learning about health and safety as you talk to learners about, and ask learners to talk about, electrical safety.

Homework ideas

Learners might carry out the survey from the Think like a scientist activity at home. They could note answers from one or two family members.

Learners could design an electrical safety poster for home. This could be general or for the kitchen.

Topic worksheets

Worksheets 6.2A, 6.2B and 6.2C

Worksheet 6.2A asks learners to circle dangers in the bathroom.

Worksheet 6.2B asks the learner to write a list of rules for electrical safety.

Worksheet 6.2C asks learners to draw other potential dangers.

6.3 Making circuits

LEARNING PLAN

Learning objectives	Learning intention	Success criteria
2Pe.02 Recognise the components of simple circuits (limited to cells, wires and lamps). **2Pe.03** Explore the construction of simple series circuits (limited to cells, wires and lamps).	• We are going to explore making different circuits with cells, wires and lamps.	• I can use cells, wires and lamps to make electrical circuits.
2TWSp.02 Make predictions about what they think will happen. **2TWSa.01** Describe what happened during an enquiry and if it matched their predictions.	• We are going to make predictions and see if they were right.	• I can make predictions and see if they were right.
2TWSa.02 Identify simple patterns in results, for example, increasing and decreasing patterns.	• We are going to find patterns in results.	• I can find patterns in results.
2TWSc.02 Use given equipment appropriately. **2TWSc.04** Follow instructions safely when doing practical work.	• We are going to follow instructions safely when making circuits.	• I can follow instructions safely when making circuits.

LANGUAGE SUPPORT

Some of the language used around circuit making is unfamiliar, for example, conductor, and it includes scientific terms that have to be used correctly, for example, complete circuit.

Create a large circuit on a poster on the wall with wires lamp and cells. Label this clearly as a glossary of electrical words.

Link new words to familiar ones. For example, you might point out that the word circuit sounds like the word circle.

Ask learners to make a wordsearch containing key electrical terms.

CONTINUED

circuit: a circle of joined wire and electrical parts along which electricity flows

complete: no missing parts

conductor: a material through which electricity will flow

connect: to join things together

connection: a place where things (for example, two wires) join together

flow: move

lamp: gives light when it is in a circuit

Common misconceptions

Misconception	How to identify	How to overcome
That electricity comes out of both ends of a cell and crashes in the lamp to make light.	Ask learners to look at a working circuit and tell you how the electricity is moving.	Make it clear that electricity flows around a circuit. Demonstrate this with role plays as below.
Some learners may think that the colour of the plastic coating on the wire is significant in some way.	When making circuits, you may hear learners refer to the colour of the wire 'we must have red wire like the teacher did'.	Explain that the colour of the wire is only important in bigger complicated circuits and with mains electricity. In our circuits, the metal in the wire is the same so we can use any colour.
Sometimes learners will try to keep wires very short so as not to 'leak' electricity.	You may see learners making very small circuits. Ask them why.	You can explain that electricity cannot leak out of wires. Wire length on our table top circuits is not an issue.

Starter ideas

1 Role play of electricity (10–15 minutes)

Resources: Two signs reading cell and lamp, masking tape or chalk

Description: Use masking tape or chalk to make a large circle on the floor. At one point on the line, place the sign reading cell and on the other side of the shape the label reading lamp. Ask a group of 10 to 20 learners to stand on the circle all facing the same way (either clockwise or anticlockwise). Explain that they will represent the electricity flowing through the circuit. Ask one extra learner to be the cell. This learner will stand by the cell sign and gently push the learners, each learner represents one 'bit' of electricity (an electron), moving around the circuit. Ask learners, when they reach the lamp, to smile to show the lamp is glowing. Now ask everyone to slowly start moving together around the circuit. Check that learners understand about the gentle push and smile. Ask any learners in the audience to watch and think of features they like. Ask the role players to 'freeze'. Now ask several role players what has happened, where have they been? What did they do? Restart the learners, but now explain that the cell is getting tired, it cannot push so hard, the flow of electricity is reducing, now even more tired and now the cell is 'flat', it has no more push, there is no electrical flow. Ask the learners to explain what happened. Emphasise that it is the cell that pushes and that eventually it has no more energy and so is exhausted. (If you carry this role play out on the playground with chalk on the floor the learners may continue the lesson at playtime.)

Listen to questions learners ask, as these may reveal misconceptions, for example, that electricity is used up in the lamp (the electricity is used up in the cell which pushes the flow).

2 Inside a flashlight (10 minutes)

Resources: A flashlight

Description: Explain that, because a flashlight uses cells, it is safe to take it apart. We must not do this mains powered appliances even if they are unplugged, because some parts can store a lot of electricity. Explain that learners should only do this with an adult. Ask learners what they think will be inside a flashlight (they may say, wires, batteries). Open the flashlight and remove the cells. Explain that we call these cells. Point to the metal spring, explaining that it is a wire, but it is in the shape of a spring to hold the cells in place. There may be wires to see, or strips of copper metal. These carry the electricity up the lamp. You may be able to show learners the lamp, the surrounding mirror and the glass or plastic cover over the lamp. Ask learners what the parts do, for example, the mirror reflects light out of the front of the flashlight. Explain that the parts have to go back together in the right way or the flashlight will not work.

Learners may think that electricity comes out of both ends of a cell and crashes in the lamp to make light. Make it clear that electricity flows around a circuit.

Main teaching ideas

1   Activity 1: Make a circuit (20–30 minutes)

Learning intention: We are going to explore making different circuits with cells, wires and lamps.

We are going to follow instructions safely when making circuits.

Resources: Learner's Book, for each learner or pair: a cell, two wires, a lamp and lamp holder; or pictures of wires, cells, lamps in holders (optional), Workbook 6.3 Focus and Practice (optional), scissors, paper, glue, dice, Digital Classroom manipulative: Can you build a circuit? (optional)

Description: Ask the learners to look at the pictures in the Learner's Book showing the equipment and a circuit. The Workbook 6.3 Focus exercise might be used here to reinforce the names and function of the electrical components. Ask learners to use the equipment they have to make a complete working circuit. Some learners may need support, but try to allow them to explore the equipment.

> **Digital Classroom:** If you have access to the Digital Classroom component, you might use the manipulative 'Can you build a circuit?' at this point, allowing learners to make a circuit on screen. The i button will explain how to use the manipulative.

Ask learners to use a finger to follow the flow of electricity around the circuit. Emphasise the need

for a complete circuit. For example, ask learners to break or disconnect the circuit and then re-connect it so that it works again. Learners can use pictures to record the circuits they have made, or design circuits they plan to make. Learners can cut out pictures of the circuit parts and stick them together to form a complete circuit. Another option is for two learners to use a die to play a game. The learners cut out pictures of all the circuit parts and take it turns to throw the die. Whenever they throw an even number, they can add a part to the circuit.

You might use the Workbook 6.3 Practice exercise at this point, which asks learners to identify circuits that would or would not work.

> **Practical guidance:** If at first circuits do not work, try swapping the cell for another you know contains electricity. After that, you should test the lamps. See the advice in the subject background guidance above.

> **Assessment ideas:** Ask learners to cut out pictures of the circuit parts and assemble a complete circuit.

2   Think like a scientist: Do more lamps mean brighter lamps? (15–20 minutes)

Learning intention: We are going to explore making different circuits with cells, wires and lamps.

We are going to make predictions and see if they were right.

We are going to follow instructions safely when making circuits.

Resources: Learner's Book, wires, two cells, three lamp holders, three lamps (of equal voltage rating) per learner, pair or small group, plus some spares of each component

Description: Ask learners to make a circuit with five wires, two cells, two lamp holders and two lamps. Ask learners what will happen to the brightness of the lamps if you add an extra lamp. Ask them to make a prediction for two, three, four and even five lamps. Learners should test these circuits and record the predictions and results. After the testing, ask learners to report their results. They should find that as they add lamps to the circuit, the lamps shine less brightly. Discuss whether the results showed a pattern.

> **Practical guidance:** If possible, have learners working individually or in pairs. If you don't have enough equipment for this, small groups will do.

> **Practical guidance:** Make sure that when cells are connected to one another, they are arranged so that the negative terminal connects to the positive terminal of the next cell. If learners have difficulty holding the cells, then use sticky tape to stick the cells on to card. Try to ensure that all the lamps are of equal voltage rating (printed on the side of the lamp), for example, 1.5 V or 2.5 V. If this is not the case, then the pattern may not be clear.

> **Differentiation ideas:** Less confident learners may require more guidance. You could provide an example circuit or drawing of a circuit on their table to copy.

More confident learners could use more lamps, or predict what would happen with more lamps.

> **Assessment ideas:** Can learners point to the circuit and describe a flow of electricity around the circuit? On a picture of the circuit, can they draw arrows to show this?

3 Activity 2: Why are wires made of metal? (20–30 minutes)

Learning intention: We are going to explore making different circuits with cells, wires and lamps.

We are going to follow instructions safely when making circuits.

Resources: Learner's Book, cell, wires or crocodile clips, lamp and lamp holder, materials to test, for example, a metal nail, a plastic straw, paper, a wooden stick, a metal paper clip, a leaf, a metal spoon, a piece of fabric, metal foil, cell holders, crocodile clips, copies of table in Learner's Book, Workbook 6.3 Challenge

Description: Explain that the metal in a wire conducts electricity, so we can test to see which materials conduct electricity and which do not. Show learners an incomplete circuit like the one in Activity 2 in the Learner's Book. Ask a learner to select a material to test and to predict what will happen when they hold the material across the gap, or clip the material to each crocodile clip. Ask learners to observe and then explain what happened. Repeat the test, but using a metal object. Ask learners to explain what is happening. For example, when we place an electrical conductor across the gap, the electricity flows around the circuit and lights the lamp.

Ask learners to make predictions and to complete a table like the one in the Learner's Book.

> **Differentiation ideas:** Provide more or less challenge with a larger or smaller set of materials.

> **Assessment ideas:** Ask a learner to hold a piece of plastic insulated wire. Ask them to explain why metal is used for the wire and plastic to cover the wire.

4 Activity 3: Do more cells make lamps brighter? (15–20 minutes)

Learning intention: We are going to explore making different circuits with cells, wires and lamps.

We are going to follow instructions safely when making circuits.

Resources: Learner's Book, two wires, two cells, one lamp holder, one lamp per individual, pair or small group, pictures of wires, cells, lamps in a lamp holders (optional), Workbook 6.3 Challenge

Description: Ask learners individually, or in pairs, to make a circuit again using one cell, two wires a lamp and lamp holder. Ask learners to predict what will happen if they add another cell (these must be connected + to –, if learners get this wrong, it is not dangerous, but the circuit is unlikely to work). Ask learners to predict and then to add another cell the same way around as the first one (+ to –). Ask learners to report what happens (the lamp should glow more brightly). By the end of this activity, the learners should be confident trying out different ideas and see that as more cells are added lamps will glow more brightly.

Pictures of the circuit parts might be helpful here for learners to plan and/or record circuits.

At this point, you might use the Workbook 6.3 Challenge exercise, which asks questions about circuits with different numbers of cells.

> **Practical guidance:** If possible, have learners working individually or in pairs. If you don't have enough equipment for this small groups will do.

Learners may want to add more cells, but this may lead to the lamps 'blowing' (this just means that the tiny filament in the lamp overheats and stops working – it is not dangerous). It is a good idea to explain that this is not dangerous, but can be expensive and wasteful.

> **Differentiation ideas:** Support less confident learners by providing a ready-made circuit for them to copy or drawing of a circuit to copy.

Challenge more confident learners by asking for an explanation. For example, that the extra cell provides more electricity or push which makes the lamp glow more brightly.

> **Assessment ideas:** Show learners a circuit with one cell and lamp. Ask them say if adding another lamp will make the lamps glow more brightly.

Plenary ideas

1 Holding hands circuit model (10 minutes)

Resources: A label with 'lamp' written on it and one with 'cell', Worksheet 6.3A, 6.3B, 6.3C

Description: Arrange six to ten learners in a circle holding hands. Give one learner the cell label. Choose a learner on the opposite side of the circle and give him/her the lamp label. Ask the 'cell' learner to repeatedly squeeze the hand of the learner to their left and ask the learners to pass this on going around and around. While this happens the 'lamp' learner smiles to show they are 'shining'. We see the circuit working, electricity is flowing and the lamp working. Gently hold and pull apart two learners hands so the 'circuit' is broken. The squeeze cannot be passed on. The 'lamp' child stops smiling, the lamp is not shining. Ask the learners what just happened. For example, the circuit was broken, the electricity could not flow and the lamp is now not glowing/ not bright.

You might make use of the worksheets at this point to assess learners' understanding of circuits. You can use the worksheet in different ways, the options below are progressively more challenging.

Worksheet 6.3A

Ask learners to use equipment to copy these circuit pictures to see if they work. Ask learners to put a tick by the circuits that worked and a cross by the circuits that did not work.

Worksheet 6.3B

Ask learners to put a tick by the complete circuits that will work and a cross by those that are not complete and will not work. Then ask learners to add arrows to the complete circuits to show the flow

of the electricity around the circuit (the direction does not matter with this age group).

Worksheet 6.3C

Ask learners to explain (verbally or in writing) why each circuit works/does not work. They could cut each out stick them into a book and write next to the diagram. Ask learners to say and draw how they would change the circuit to make each circuit work.

> **Assessment ideas:** While making the model above, ask individuals to tell you what is happening.

> **Reflection ideas:** Ask learners: Does a model like this help me learn science?

Can I improve on this model?

2 Does a long wire lose electricity? (15 minutes)

Resources: Cell, cell holder, lamp, lamp holder, crocodile clips, a very long wire (at least 3 to 4 metres)

Description: Explain that some people think that a longer wire will lose electricity. What do learners think? Ask two learners to make a circuit without the very long wire. Now ask what will happen if we include a much longer wire into the circuit. Some learners may think that electricity will 'be lost' or 'get weak' on the journey. Ask the learners to add in the very long wire and, if possible, arrange the circuit in a circle which now travels around a table or part of the classroom. Connect the circuit and observe that the lamp is just as bright as it was.

> **Assessment ideas:** Ask learners how they might make a circuit to light a lamp over the classroom door and have the cell at floor level.

> **Reflection ideas:** Ask learners: If the wire stretched further, for example, to the next town or village, do you think the result would be the same? (The result would be the same. However, if the wire were hundreds of miles long there would be a small loss of electricity.)

CROSS-CURRICULAR LINKS

Link this topic to other learning about health and safety as you talk to learners about, and ask learners to talk about, electrical safety.

Homework ideas

Give learners pictures of the circuit parts and ask them to design a circuit at home.

Give learners the outline of a car and ask them to draw a circuit for a light on the roof (like a police car) using a cell, wires and a lamp.

Topic worksheets

Worksheets 6.3A, 6.3B and 6.3C

Worksheet 6.3A asks learners to use equipment to copy the circuit pictures to see if they work. It also asks learners to put a tick by the circuits that worked and a cross by the circuits that did not work.

Worksheet 6.3B asks learners to put a tick by the complete circuits that will work and a cross by those that are not complete and will not work.

Worksheet 6.3C asks learners to explain (verbally or in writing) why each circuit works/does not work. They could cut each out stick them into a book and write next to the diagram. It then asks learners to say and draw how they would change the circuit to make each circuit work.

PROJECT: INVENT A NEW ELECTRICAL APPLIANCE

2SIC.02 Talk about how science explains how objects they use, or know about, work.

This project allows learners to think of new possible appliances that might use electricity. Some examples are given in the Learner's Book. Others might include: electric scissors, an electric umbrella, a fan that plays music, electric shoes, a heated hat, etc. Almost any safe suggestion can be accepted.

Ask the learners to think about how and when they would use the appliance, whether it would be mains-powered or cell-powered, and where it would have a switch.

> Glossary

absorb – when water soaks into the material

absorbent – something that soaks up water and other liquids, not waterproof

adult – an animal that is fully grown and could become a parent

age – how many years a living thing has been alive

anti-clockwise – turning the opposite way to a clock's hands

attract – draw something towards it

away – moving away from something is getting less close to it

baby – a very young animal

bird – an animal with feathers and wings, most birds can fly

block graph – a way of showing results that uses squares or blocks instead of numbers

brakes – the parts of a bike or other vehicle that make it slow down

bright – a bright object gives off a lot of light, opposite to dull

calcium – something found in milk and other dairy food that helps teeth grow strong

calf – a young elephant, cow or whale is called a calf

canine – a type of tooth with a pointed top for gripping food

cell (electrical) – a source of energy or electricity that can power a circuit

characteristics – what a material or a living thing is like, for example, a material could be flexible or rigid, an animal could have two legs or four legs

chick – young birds are called chicks

circuit – a circle of joined wire and electrical parts along which electricity flows

clean – not dirty

clues – things we observe which help us understand

compare – to look at two things and find things that are similar and different

complete – no missing parts

conductor – a material through which electricity will flow

connect – to join things together

connection – a place where things (for example, two wires) join together

cotton – a fluffy white material that comes from a plant and is made into a fabric

crack – a broken part of a material

cub – a young bear, wolf, lion or tiger is called a cub

dairy – food that has milk in it or food that is made from milk

dangerous – it may hurt you

dark – less light or no light

daylight – the light we get from the Sun

daytime – the hours of the day when we get light from the Sun

dentist – a doctor who looks after people's teeth

describe – use words to say what something is like

desert – a very dry place with little or no living things

diagram – a drawing that shows important information and explains this with labels and arrows, lines and text

diet – the food we eat

direction – a path towards or away from something

discovery – something found for the first time

droppings – solid waste made by animals

dull – something that light does not bounce off, not shiny

egg – a shell or case made by female animals, each contains young

electric shock – a dangerous amount of electricity in a person's body

electrical appliance – a device that uses electricity to work

electricity – we use it to make things work like TVs, computers, phones

environment – the natural and man-made space and things around you

exercise – moving around using your muscles

explain – to make something clear

explosive – a material that will blow things apart

famous – well-known by many people

fast, faster – to take little time to move to a new place

feathers – feathers cover the skins of birds and help them to fly

fingerprint – the pattern of lines in the skin of your fingers

flashlight – an electric light that you can hold in your hand

flexible – something that can bend, squash or twist, not rigid

flow – move

fluoride – something found in some toothpastes which makes teeth stronger

force – a push or a pull

fur – soft hair that covers the skin of some animals

germs – very small living things that can make you ill

glass – a clear material we use to make windows

gravel – small pieces of rock

grow/growth – changes that happen as living things get older

gums – the part of the mouth that teeth grow from

habitat – the place a living thing finds everything it needs to grow and have young

headache – when your head hurts

heart – part of our bodies that pumps blood around our body to help keep us alive

height – how far from the bottom to the top of an object

hide – keeping out of sight

home – the place an animal sleeps, feels safe and cares for its young

human – a person

identical – exactly the same

ill/illness – not feeling well, not being well

incisor – a type of tooth with a flat sharp top for biting food

information – facts about something

inherit – getting a characteristic from a parent when you are born

insect – a small animal with three body parts and six legs

invention – something new created by a person

investigate – to do a test or experiment to find something out

label – words added to a picture to give information

lamp – gives light when it is in a circuit

launch – when something starts moving into the air or into water

light source – an object which makes light

liquid – a material that can flow and be poured, for example, water is a liquid

litter – something dropped on the ground which should be put in a bin

local – the area around you

mains electricity – very powerful electricity we use in buildings

mammal – an animal that has hair or fur and has live babies instead of laying eggs

material – a substance used to make something

measure – to find the size or amount of something, for example length or time

melt – to change from solid to liquid

mine – hole dug to extract rocks or minerals

mixture – something that is made by putting different materials together

model – a copy we make (often smaller) of a real thing

molar – a type of tooth with a wide lumpy top for chewing food

Moon – large body which orbits Earth and which, on most nights, reflects light to Earth

muscles – part of our bodies that can make us move

natural – can be found in nature, not made by people

nature reserve – a place which is made to be a good habitat for plants and animals

night time – the hours of darkness

object – something made of a material that you can see or touch.

oil – a black liquid material that is found underground that can burn

old/older – an animal that has been alive for a long time

paper – a material we can use to write on

parent – an animal's mother or father

pattern – a change that is similar each time

pedals – the parts of a bike you push with your feet to make it move

photograph – a picture made by a camera

pictogram – a way of showing results that uses pictures instead of numbers plastic – a material that comes in many different colours and shapes

plug – a connection to mains electricity

position – an object's place in the physical world

power station – a factory that makes electricity

pretend – imagine something

property/properties – what something is like, for example, smooth and shiny are properties of glass

protect – to take care of something or someone

pull/pulls – to try to move something towards you

push/pushes – to try to move something away from you

quarry – a place where the surface rocks are removed so that rock from just below the surface can be dug out

record – to draw or write what happened

recycle – reuse a material so that it does not get dumped

reflect – light changing direction after hitting a surface

results – what you observe or measure in an investigation

rigid – something that keeps its shape and is not easy to bend, squash or twist, not flexible

robot – an appliance that can do things by following instructions

rock – a hard material that comes from the Earth's surface

rocked – something that moves from side to side

rocket – something that can fly to into space

rough – something is bumpy, not flat, not smooth

rubber – a material that can bend easily and comes from the rubber tree

safe – not dangerous

sample – a piece of a material

sand – loose yellow or brown material made up of very small pieces of rock

scare – frighten

shape – the outline of an object, for example, square, curved or flat

shine – making or reflecting light

shiny – something that light bounces off, not dull

sick – being sick is when your body pushes everything in your tummy out through your mouth

slide – to move something from side to side

slow down, get slower – when something starts to move less quickly

slow, slower – to take a long time to move to a new place

smooth – something that is flat, not bumpy, not rough

solid – a material that keeps its shape and does not flow

speed – how fast something is moving

speed up, get faster – when something starts to move more quickly

spin – turning on the spot

squashing – changing the shape of a material by pushing, when something gets shorter

star – a very large burning object in the sky which is very far away and so appears very small

steel – a shiny metal through which electricity will flow

stones – small rocks

stretch – change the shape of a material by pulling, when something gets longer

stripes – a pattern of lines

strong – something that is not easy to break, not weak

sundial – a device which casts a shadow indicating the time of day

sunrise – as the Sun appears to rise from the horizon and appear in the sky as the Earth turns

sweat – when your skin become wet because you are hot or ill

swirl – make a liquid spin

switch – a device to control the flow of electricity (on/off)

table – a grid of squares we use to write or draw results

toothpaste – something to put on a toothbrush to help clean teeth and make them strong

towards – moving towards something is getting closer to it

tracks – marks made by an animal as it moves

transparent – a material you can see through clearly

turn – when something moving changes to move on a different path

twins – two people or animals with the same mother who were born at the same time

Venn diagram – a picture used for sorting with two circles that overlap wall socket – the place you connect some electrical appliances to the mains

water – a clear liquid material that we need to drink, the sea and rivers are water

waterproof – a material that does not let water through

weak – something that is easy to break, not strong

wire – a long thin piece of metal

wood – a material that comes from the trunk of a tree

young (adj) – an animal that has not been alive for long

young (noun) – an animal's babies are called its young